Presented to
The Kansas School of Religion
Library
From
Spiritual Assembly of
Baha'i's
Lawrence, Kansas 1975

BAHÁ'U'LLÁH

THE WORD MADE FLESH

By the same author

'ABDU'L-BAHÁ (*George Ronald, London, 1971*)
The Centre of the Covenant
of Bahá'u'lláh

EDWARD GRANVILLE BROWNE
AND THE BAHÁ'Í FAITH (*George Ronald, London, 1970*)

BAHÁ'U'LLÁH

a brief life, followed by an essay on the Manifestation of God entitled

THE WORD MADE FLESH

by

H. M. BALYUZI

GEORGE RONALD
LONDON

First published by
George Ronald
17–21 Sunbeam Road, London NW10

Reprinted 1968, 1970 and 1972

ISBN 0 85398 014 4

COMPOSED IN 11 ON 13 GARAMOND AND PRINTED
IN ENGLAND BY THE WHITEFRIARS PRESS LTD

CONTENTS

BAHÁ'U'LLÁH

'The humanitarian and spiritual principles enunciated decades ago in the darkest East by Bahá'u'lláh and moulded by Him into a coherent scheme are one after the other being taken by a world unconscious of their source as the marks of progressive civilization. And the sense that mankind has broken with the past and that the old guidance will not carry it through the emergencies of the present has filled with uncertainty and dismay all thoughtful men save those who have learned to find in the story of Bahá'u'lláh the meaning of all the prodigies and portents of our time.' *Shoghi Effendi*

The towering grandeur and the tender beauty of the life of a Manifestation of God cannot be comprehended by events usually associated with a saintly life. The immensity of such a life presents itself in that mysterious influence which it exerts over countless lives, an influence which functions not through social status and prestige, wealth, secular power or worldly dominion; indeed not even through a medium of mere superior knowledge and intellectual achievement.

The Manifestation of God is the Archetype, and His life is the supreme pattern. His vision, not arrested by time and space, encompasses the future as well as the past. He is the only and the necessary link between one period of social evolution and another. Without Him history is meaningless and coordination is impossible. Furthermore, the Manifestation of God releases deep reservoirs of spiritual power and quickens the forces latent in humanity. By Him, and by Him alone, can Man attain 'second birth'.

Mírzá Ḥusayn-'Alí, later surnamed Bahá'u'lláh, was born on November 12th, 1817, in Ṭihrán, the capital of Persia. His father, Mírzá Buzurg of Núr, held a responsible post in the ministerial circle of the Sháh's court. All accounts of Bahá'u'lláh's childhood indicate that from His earliest years He possessed remarkable and very unusual powers. At the age of seven, He appeared before the Sháh, to argue a case on behalf of His father, and proved His suit. His character endeared Him not only to His kinsmen and immediate entourage, but to strangers as well. The minister was fully conscious of the extraordinary powers of his Son, although the destiny of the Child could not but be unknown to him. Bahá'u'lláh grew up in the environs of the court, amidst riches and great comfort. But when His father died, and the post left vacant in the court was offered to Him, He refused to accept it. The Grand Vizier, we are told, said that Mírzá Ḥusayn-'Alí was intended for a work of greater magnitude, and the arena of government was too small a field for His capacities.

In those days, the nobility of Írán cared little for the sciences and the arts of the learned. Beyond excellent calligraphy, a knowledge of the sacred scriptures of Islám, and a well-founded acquaintance with the works of such prominent figures in Persian literature as Rúmí, Firdausí, Sa'dí and Ḥáfiz, they generally knew but little. There were notable exceptions of course. Bahá'u'lláh was more than an exception. Although untutored, He plunged freely and naturally into such talks and discussions as were considered to be the domain of the theologian and the scholar. Time and again He astounded the doctors of religion and the learned of the land by His clear reasoning and irrefutable logic. Oftentimes a person encroaching upon precincts reserved to others becomes presumptuous, arrogant, and haughty. Bahá'u'lláh was modest, genial, and forbearing.

This youthful scion of a house of nobility had an overwhelming passion for justice. He deserted the court to tend the oppressed and the aggrieved. Not once did He hesitate to champion the cause of the poor and the fallen who turned to Him for succour and help. None who deserved was refused. Thus passed the days of His Youth, until a day came when an emissary set out with a letter to seek Him, and the very qualities that made Him a haven and refuge, and raised Him in the esteem of His fellow-men, convinced that emissary that the Son of the late minister from Núr was indeed the Exalted Person intended to receive the letter of the Báb.

On May 22nd, 1844, a young merchant of Shíráz, whose name was Siyyid 'Alí-Muḥammad, revealed Himself to a seeker as that Deliverer Whom the world of Islám anxiously awaited. An independent Manifestation of God and the Harbinger of a greater Manifestation, He took the title of the Báb, meaning 'Gate'. His primary mission was to awaken the slumbering people of Írán, and to warn the followers of the Faith of Muḥammad—a Faith by then, alas, laden with abuses. The Báb sent Mullá Ḥusayn, that seeker who was the first to believe in Him, to the capital, and entrusted Him with a letter for an unnamed Person, supreme in heavenly rank. Mullá Ḥusayn reached Ṭihrán, determined to let Providence guide his steps. He searched indomitably, but in vain. At last a visitor came to him, whose home-town was Núr in Mázindarán, the home of Bahá'u'lláh's family. In the course of conversation Mullá Ḥusayn inquired about the sons of the late Mírzá Buzurg, the minister from Núr. Thus he heard of Mírzá Ḥusayn-'Alí, and eagerly asked for more information. And when the full story was unfolded to him, he knew in an instant that he had found the unnamed Person Who was to receive the letter sent by the Báb. He had come to the end of his quest. In due course, the Báb's Epistle was taken to Bahá'u'lláh, Who accepted the Truth that it contained. Thus at the age of twenty-seven, the Son of the minister, Who had withdrawn from the life of the court, the brilliant nobleman Whose sense of justice was a byword amongst all who knew Him, Whose knowledge, eloquence and lovable nature were exemplary, put Himself on the side of a religious renaissance that was bound to excite the hatred of the ruling classes of the realm.

The Báb had implicit assurance that the nobleman of Núr would ultimately wield the sceptre of supreme authority. It was the Báb Who assigned to Him the designation Bahá'u'lláh—the Glory of God. One cannot fail to perceive the affection, the respect and the attachment which the Báb showed towards

Bahá'u'lláh, sentiments which found no parallel in His regard for the rest of His able and devout followers.

Soon after His conversion, Bahá'u'lláh travelled to His native province on the shores of the Caspian Sea, to promote the Message of the Báb. He was highly esteemed in Mázindarán, and therefore apt to arouse controversy in orthodox camps. He challenged a clergyman of considerable local standing to refute His proofs, but the latter, finding himself unequal to the task, evaded the issue.

Then, in the middle part of 1848, occurred the Conference of Badasht. The followers of the Báb, harassed and persecuted, witnessing their Master in prison and cruel detention, came to meet in a secluded part of Khurásán, in the northeast of Persia, to examine the problems facing them as a hounded community and adherents of a proscribed Faith. There was present the learned and confident Quddús, the most venerated of the first disciples of the Báb—those who sought Him and found Him and believed in Him, and were named by Him 'The Letters of the Living'. There was the silver-tongued and courageous poetess Qurratu'l-'Ayn, later known as Ṭáhirih, another of the Letters of the Living and the only one of that band of eighteen who never met the Báb, but believed in Him from afar and sent Him her eloquent homage through a kinsman who was setting out on his quest. Bahá'u'lláh, too, was there. Throughout the discussion He maintained a dignified silence, but when the Conference reached its end, His was the decisive and the undisputed word.

The Bábís had not yet fully grasped the significance of the Báb's revelation. Qurratu'l-'Ayn discarded her veil and appeared in the assemblage of men with face uncovered, as a token of new birth and a new day. In that gathering she raised her voice in defiance of superstition, prejudice and blind imitation. Quddús, deeply versed in theology, and firm in his beliefs, would not sanction the advanced measures advocated by Qurratu'l-'Ayn. Now Bahá'u'lláh threw the weight of His innate wisdom into the balance. The Báb, He told the assembly, was the Founder of a new Dispensation, and stood in the same heavenly lineage as Muḥammad, Jesus and Moses. A few half-hearted souls left disgustedly, but the great majority were confirmed in their faith. When the Báb heard of the outcome of the Conference of Badasht, His delight was immense.

From Badasht, Bahá'u'lláh returned to Ṭihrán. Not long after, He visited Mullá Ḥusayn, who, with more than three hundred Bábís had sought refuge in the shrine of Shaykh Ṭabarsí in the forests of Mázindarán. Mullá Ḥusayn built defences around the shrine, and was eventually joined by Quddús. The infuriated clergy stormed the government to send a punitive expedition against that hounded band of innocent and God-fearing men. Troops marched and laid siege to the fortress which sheltered the Bábís. Hearing the news, Bahá'u'lláh left promptly for the Fort of Ṭabarsí, wishing to share the calamities of His brethren in faith. Providence had deemed that the heroic defenders of Shaykh Ṭabarsí should seal the Covenant of the Báb with their blood, and that Bahá'u'lláh should be preserved for a far greater purpose in days to come. He was stopped on His way, by the Governor's men, and taken to the town of Ámul. The doctors of religion preached death, and the mob thirsted for violence. In order to appease the populace, the deputy-governor decided to inflict some kind of punishment on the members of Bahá'u'lláh's retinue. Bahá'u'lláh offered Himself in lieu of His friends, and voluntarily drew the wrath of the mob upon His own Person. He was bastinadoed.

On July 9th, 1850, the gracious and gentle Báb was shot in the public square of Tabríz. His breast, that heaved not but in adoration of God, was made the target of bullets. Bahá'u'lláh had sent Sulaymán Khán, a brilliant and brave youth, to rescue the mangled remains of the Báb from the fury of the foe. And then He arranged for the concealment of the remains in order to protect them from the evil designs of the oppressors. For more than fifty years they were hidden from the knowledge of friends and enemies alike. Today they rest on Mount Carmel, in a beautiful mausoleum under a golden dome.

Not only did the Báb quaff the cup of martyrdom, but His able and selfless lieutenants were one by one hunted down with brutal hatred—Mullá Ḥusayn, Quddús, the erudite and fearless Vaḥíd of Dáráb, the indomitable Ḥujjat of Zanján, all murdered and gone. In the length and breadth of Írán the Bábís had no peace, no security, no right to life itself. How long can a mutilated and agonised community bear and sustain the severe impact of continuous shocks! Bahá'u'lláh's arduous task had already begun. In Him were centred all those highest qualities, human and divine, that went to make the Báb and Quddús. On Him, and Him alone, depended the fate of the Bábís. It was to Him that the Báb had sent His seals, pen, and papers, a symbolic act of untold significance.

In June, 1851, Bahá'u'lláh travelled to 'Iráq. There the Bábís lived in comparative safety, but were distracted and forlorn. Bahá'u'lláh refortified their faith, and gave them fresh hope. No sooner had He returned to Ṭihrán than the storm broke out again. It was more than a storm. It was a holocaust.

The Bábís presented, indeed, a sad spectacle in this period of their short but eventful history. Their morale was impaired and their energy sapped. The fickle and the timid amongst them could see no redeeming hand, no prospect of emancipation. Two irresponsible young men, driven to despair, decided to avenge their Master and their martyred brethren. To them the source of persecution and tyranny seemed to be no other than the person of the Sovereign—the Sháh, in whose hand was the power to give them justice. The Sháh, they argued in their tormented minds, had not exercised his sovereign authority in favour of their maligned and oppressed community, and therefore he had to pay the supreme penalty. So deranged were their faculties that they did not put in their pistols proper bullets for killing a man.

On August 12th, 1852, they ventured upon their insane attempt and failed. The Sháh received only superficial injuries. The would-be murderers were not given the chance of a trial, and were summarily dealt with. But the matter did not end there. The enemies of the Báb had found their golden opportunity to exterminate His followers. Here at last, they frenziedly declaimed, was the proof of a deadly menace to the State.

Bahá'u'lláh was, at this moment, staying in a summer residence in the vicinity of the capital. His friends warned Him of the engulfing tide. They offered to hide Him from the wrath of His ill-wishers. But he remained calm and composed. He had nothing to fear, and the next day He rode towards the camp of the Sháh. The news of His approach confounded the enemy. Whilst they were plotting His arrest, and starting to search for Him, He was coming to them, of His own accord. But when had Bahá'u'lláh ever shown fear or panic?

They laid their rough hands upon His Person. On the road to the dungeon in Ṭihrán, a big crowd gathered to jeer at Him and to heap insults upon Him. He Who had been their friend and defender, their shield and support in need, was now the victim of their blazing hatred.

People did the same to Jesus. On Palm Sunday they went out to greet Him. They gave Him a royal welcome. And Jerusalem echoed with 'Hosanna to the Son of David'. 'Blessed is He,' they cried, 'that cometh in the Name of the Lord; Hosanna in the Highest.' A few days later, in the courtyard of Pontius Pilate, they were given a choice. Which should die?

Barrabas, the proved and convicted criminal, or Jesus, the Light of the World? They asked for the death of Jesus. They rejected the Christ. 'Crucify Him,' they cried.

Thus has the world ever treated its true friend.

Among the crowd, which hurled abuse at Bahá'u'lláh and pelted Him with stones, was an old woman. She stepped forward with a stone in her hand to strike at Him. Although frenzied with rage, her steps were too weak for the pace of the procession. 'Give me a chance to fling my stone in His face,' she pleaded with the guard. Bahá'u'lláh turned to them and said, 'Suffer not this woman to be disappointed. Deny her not what she regards as a meritorious act in the sight of God.' Such was the measure of His compassion.

About the attempt on the life of the Sháh, Bahá'u'lláh writes in His *Epistle to the Son of the Wolf:*

> 'By the righteousness of God! We were in no wise connected with that evil deed, and Our innocence was indisputably established by the tribunals. Nevertheless, they apprehended Us, and from Níyávarán, which was then the residence of His Majesty, conducted Us, on foot and in chains, with bared head and bare feet, to the dungeon of Ṭihrán. A brutal man, accompanying Us on horseback, snatched off Our hat, whilst We were being hurried along by a troop of executioners and officials. We were consigned for four months to a place foul beyond comparison. As to the dungeon in which this Wronged One and others similarly wronged were confined, a dark and narrow pit were preferable. Upon Our arrival We were first conducted along a pitch-black corridor, from whence We descended three steep flights of stairs to the place of confinement assigned to Us. The dungeon was wrapped in thick darkness, and Our fellow-prisoners numbered nearly a hundred and fifty souls: thieves, assassins and highwaymen. Though crowded, it had no other outlet than the passage by which We entered. No pen can depict that place, nor any tongue describe its loathsome smell. Most of these men had neither clothes nor bedding to lie

on. God alone knoweth what befell Us in that most foul-smelling and gloomy place!'[1]

The prison cell in which Bahá'u'lláh was confined, together with many other Bábís, was a grim, dark and stench-laden pit that once had served as a reservoir for a public bath, and to which the worst criminals were now consigned. Around His neck they placed one of the two most dreaded chains in the whole land. Under its ponderous weight His whole frame was bent. In that same book, *Epistle to the Son of the Wolf*, Bahá'u'lláh speaks of those awesome chains:

> 'Shouldst thou at sometime happen to visit the dungeon of His Majesty the Sháh, ask the director and chief jailer to show thee those two chains, one of which is known as Qará-Guhar, and the other as Salásil. I swear by the Day-Star of Justice that for four months this Wronged One was tormented and chained by one or the other of them. "My grief exceedeth all the woes to which Jacob gave vent, and all the afflictions of Job are but a part of My sorrows!"'[2]

Nabíl, the immortal historian of the Bahá'í Faith, recounts in his work the words which he himself heard from Bahá'u'lláh, describing the torments of those days:

'We were all huddled together in one cell, our feet in stocks, and around our necks fastened the most galling of chains. The air we breathed was laden with the foulest of impurities, while the floor on which we sat was covered with filth and infested with vermin. No ray of light was allowed to penetrate that pestilential dungeon or to warm its icy coldness. We were placed in two rows, each facing the other. We had taught them to repeat certain verses which, every night, they chanted with extreme fervour. "God is sufficient unto me; He verily is the All-sufficing!" one row would intone, while the other would reply: "In Him let the trusting trust." The chorus of these gladsome voices would continue to peal out until the early hours of the morning. Their reverberation would fill the dungeon, and, piercing its massive walls, would reach the ears of Náṣiri'd-Dín Sháh, whose palace was not far distant from the place where we were imprisoned. "What means this sound?" he was reported to have exclaimed. "It is the anthem the Bábís are intoning in their prison," they replied. The Sháh made no further remarks, nor did he attempt to restrain the enthusiasm which his prisoners, despite the horrors of their confinement, continued to display.'[3]

Day by day an official would come to the prison and call out the names of those who were to meet their martyr's death on that day. And out would walk those whose names were called, with firm steps and shining brows. Hundreds of Bábís died in that blood-bath of 1852, after being subjected to excruciating tortures.

One of that glorious band was Sulaymán Khán, the same brave spirit who, at the bidding of Bahá'u'lláh, had rescued the body of the Báb. They bored nine holes in his body and placed nine lighted candles in them. Thus they paraded him in the streets, with a howling mob jeering at his heels. Sulaymán Khán was a young courtier, accustomed to power and display. On this day of his martyrdom he stopped in the midst of his tortures and exclaimed: 'What greater pomp and pageantry than those which this day accompany my progress to win the crown of glory! Glorified be the Báb, Who can kindle such devotion in the breasts of His lovers, and can endow them with a power greater than the might of kings.' As the candles flickered in his wounds, he said, 'You have long lost your sting, O flames, and have been robbed of your power to pain me. Make haste, for from your very tongues of fire I can hear the voice that calls me to my Beloved!'[4] And when one of his tormentors reviled him, he answered with these lines:

> 'Clasping in one hand the wine-cup, in one hand the Loved One's hair;
> Thus my doom would I envisage dancing through the market-square.'

Thus died Sulaymán Khán.

Another victim in this tornado was Ṭáhirih, the beautiful, talented poetess of Qazvín—the same heroic soul who, at the Conference of Badasht, raised the call of the emancipation of her sex. Now in the dead of night they strangled her and cast her body into a pit of which no trace was left. But the memory of her supreme constancy, courage and devotion will forever endure. She knew of her approaching end and was ready for it. To her hostess, the wife of the magistrate in whose custody she was placed, Ṭáhirih said on the day preceding the night of her martyrdom: 'I am preparing to meet my Beloved, and wish to free you from the cares and anxieties of my imprisonment.' She was in bridal array.

Such was the fortitude of the Bábís and such was the magnitude of their sacrifice.

For four agony-laden months Bahá'u'lláh lingered in chains, in that dismal, pestilential dungeon of Ṭihrán.

But it was in the dark of that dungeon that Bahá'u'lláh saw the Light of God shining in His own Self. He Himself gives us a vivid and overpowering account of those hours when He became conscious of His heavenly Mission.

> 'During the days I lay in the prison of Ṭihrán, though the galling weight of the chains and the stench-filled air allowed Me but little sleep, still in those infrequent moments of slumber I felt as if something flowed from the

crown of My head over My breast, even as a mighty torrent that precipitateth itself upon the earth from the summit of a lofty mountain. Every limb of My body would, as a result, be set afire. At such moments My tongue recited what no man could bear to hear.'[5]

God, in His infinite Grace, gave the world a Universal Manifestation of His Absolute Qualities and Attributes. The promise of the Báb, nay, the promise of all the Messengers of God, was fulfilled. The time, however, had not come for a public declaration. Ten more years had to elapse, before Bahá'u'lláh would announce His Manifestation to human kind.

There was no shadow of doubt that Bahá'u'lláh was not an accomplice in the attempt made on the life of the Sháh. Yet the enemies were loath to release Him, and at the same time they dared not bring Him to the scaffold. Once, poison was introduced into His food, and the effect of it remained with Him for many years. In the end He was freed and exiled from Írán. His property was confiscated, and nothing was left to Him of His wealth. The Russian minister invited Him to go to Russia where He would be assured of a free and unmolested life. Bahá'u'lláh declined the invitation, and chose to proceed to 'Iráq. On January 12th, 1853, He left Ṭihrán, never to return. With Him were the members of His family. The winter was severe. The route was over high mountains covered with deep snow, and the means of comfort were scant. Deprived of all His earthly goods, Bahá'u'lláh could not provide such facilities as would lessen the toils and hardships of that long and arduous journey. Travelling under those adverse conditions was immensely hard, and the pace was necessarily slow.

As Bahá'u'lláh neared the frontier, a period drew to its close. Were the people of Írán aware of the loss they sustained? Steeped in ignorance, sunk in bigotry, blinded by prejudice, theirs was not to see and know. And thus Bahá'u'lláh passed out of their midst. He Who once was loved and respected by rich and poor, high and low, prince and peasant alike, was now deserted by the same people on whom He had lavished mercy, love, justice, and charity at all times. Persia lost the presence of Bahá'u'lláh, but could His spirit ever be absent from that or any other land?

In the 'Epilogue' to *Nabíl's Narrative,* a history of the early days of the Cause, written by Nabíl of Zarand, and translated by Shoghi Effendi, the Guardian of the Bahá'í Faith, Shoghi Effendi thus described those tempestuous days culminating in Bahá'u'lláh's exile: 'Never had the fortunes of the Faith proclaimed by the Báb sunk to a lower ebb than when Bahá'u'lláh was banished from His native land to 'Iráq. The Cause for which the Báb had given His life, for which Bahá'u'lláh had toiled and suffered, seemed to be on the very verge of extinction. Its force appeared to have been spent, its resistance irretrievably broken. Discouragement and disasters, each more devastating in its effect than the preceding one, had succeeded one another with bewildering rapidity, sapping its vitality and dimming the hopes of its stoutest supporters.'[6]

Bahá'u'lláh arrived at Baghdád in March, 1853. His physical strength was momentarily impaired. To a casual observer He might have looked like a man approaching His end. Indeed the court and the priesthood of Írán were confident that Bahá'u'lláh was doomed to an early death and oblivion. But He survived all the hardships to which He was subjected, and as soon as He recovered from the effects of His harsh imprisonment and painful journey, He arose to reassemble and reanimate the stricken and shattered community of the Báb. That was the resolve He had come to, in the dungeon of Ṭihrán.

> 'Day and night, while confined in that dungeon,' He tells us, 'We meditated upon the deeds, the condition, and the conduct of the Bábís, wondering what could have led a people so high-minded, so noble, and of such intelligence, to perpetrate such an audacious and outrageous act against the person of His Majesty. This Wronged One, thereupon, decided to arise, after His release from prison, and undertake, with the utmost vigour, the task of regenerating this people.
>
> 'One night, in a dream, these exalted words were heard on every side: "Verily, We shall render Thee victorious by Thyself and by Thy Pen. Grieve Thou not for that which hath befallen Thee, neither be Thou afraid, for Thou art in safety. Ere long will God raise up the treasures of the earth—men who will aid Thee through Thyself and through Thy Name, wherewith God hath revived the hearts of such as have recognized Him." '[7]

The plight of the Bábís was grievous indeed. Stunned by the staggering blows dealt them by a vigilant and relentless enemy, disintegrated by factional strifes, they could not for the moment observe the guiding hand of Bahá'u'lláh. Yet, unknown to friend and foe, He was the Repository of Divine Revelation, the Vicar of God on Earth.

The Báb had clearly, and in most emphatic language, foretold the proximity of the advent of 'Him Whom God Will Make Manifest', that World Educator Who was to rear and lead humanity in the 'Day of Days'. At this period many an adventurer forwarded a claim to that station. Thus a number of the Bábís were divided into numerous parties, each supporting one of these self-appointed messiahs. The nominal head of the Bábí Community, Bahá'u'lláh's half-brother, Mírzá Yaḥyá, entitled Ṣubḥ-i-Azal or 'Morning of Eternity', was incompetent to cope with the forces of disruption. He lacked courage. At a time when Bahá'u'lláh was facing the enemy with calm fortitude, Azal was a fugitive trying to save his own life. When

Bahá'u'lláh was in chains, Azal roamed the countryside, in disguise. In the garb of a dervish, he reached Baghdád, sometime after the arrival of Bahá'u'lláh, not having raised so much as a finger in vindication of the Cause. It was Bahá'u'lláh Who had exposed Himself to the fury of the court and the clergy.

As conflicts grew and rifts widened, as baseless claims became more blatant, the hopes of the Bábí community sank lower and lower. And yet, still unknown to the Bábís as the One promised to them by the Báb, there was amongst them and suffering with them, He Who was destined to change their misery to glory, their weakness to towering strength.

No sooner had Bahá'u'lláh started upon the task of rescuing the Bábís from their waywardness, than Ṣubḥ-i-Azal, goaded by a few of the self-seeking who had chosen to make that already discredited figure the instrument of their own treacherous designs, began to obstruct Bahá'u'lláh's benevolent lead. So fierce became the opposition engineered by Azal that Bahá'u'lláh decided to retire from the scene of contention. He had no wish to add to the injuries afflicting the Bábí community. One morning His household awoke to find Him gone. He sought an abode in the mountains of Kurdistán. Such seclusion from the society of men has always occurred in the lives of the Manifestations of God. Moses went out to the desert of Sinai. Buddha sought the wilds of India. Christ walked the wilderness. Muḥammad paced the sun-baked hillocks of Arabia.

Bahá'u'lláh's self-imposed exile was a test. Were He to be the only Guide capable of showing the right path to the Bábís, the only One Who could restore to them their broken inner peace, their vision, their serenity, their faith and determination, the passage of time and His absence would prove it conclusively. And time did amply demonstrate the fact. This is how He writes of those days:

'For a number of people who have never inhaled the fragrance of justice, have raised the standard of sedition, and have leagued themselves against Us. On every side We witness the menace of their spears, and in all directions We recognize the shafts of their arrows. This, although We have never gloried in anything, nor did We seek preference over any soul. To everyone We have been a most kindly companion, a most forbearing and affectionate friend. In the company of the poor We have sought their fellowship, and amidst the exalted and learned We have been submissive and resigned. I swear by God, the one true God! grievous as have been the woes and sufferings which the hand of the enemy and the people of the Book inflicted upon Us, yet all these fade into utter nothingness when compared with that which hath befallen Us at the hand of those who profess to be Our friends.

'What more shall We say? The universe, were it to gaze with the eye of justice, would be incapable of bearing the weight of this utterance! In the early days of Our arrival in this land, when We discerned the signs of impending events, We decided, ere they happened, to retire. We betook Ourselves to the wilderness, and there, separated and alone, led for two years a life of complete solitude. From Our eyes there rained tears of anguish, and in Our bleeding heart there surged an ocean of agonizing pain. Many a night We had no food for sustenance, and many a day Our body found no rest. By Him Who hath My being between His hands! notwithstanding these showers of afflictions and unceasing calamities, Our soul was wrapt in blissful joy, and Our whole being evinced an ineffable gladness. For in Our solitude We were unaware of the harm or benefit, the health or ailment, of any soul. Alone, We communed with Our spirit, oblivious of the world and all that is therein. We knew not, however, that the mesh of divine destiny exceedeth the vastest of mortal conceptions, and the dart of His decree transcendeth the boldest of human designs. None can escape the snares He setteth, and no soul can find release except through submission to His Will. By the righteousness of God! Our withdrawal contemplated no return, and Our separation hoped for no reunion. The one object of Our retirement was to avoid becoming a subject of discord among the faithful, a source of disturbance unto Our companions, the means of injury to any soul, or the cause of sorrow to any heart. Beyond these, We cherished no other intention, and apart from them, We had no end in view. And yet, each person schemed after his own desire, and pursued his own idle fancy, until the hour when, from the Mystic Source, there came the summons bidding Us return whence We came. Surrendering Our will to His, We submitted to His injunction.'[8]

Gradually the fame of Bahá'u'lláh spread around the district of Sulaymáníyyih. None in the neighbourhood knew His identity, but all were charmed by His kindliness and wisdom. Some mistook Him for an adherent of a Súfí order. He was known by the name of Darvís͟h Muḥammad. And in a widening circle, Bag͟hdád came to hear of the wise hermit who had appeared in the mountainous regions of the north. They spoke of His knowledge, gentleness, piety and astonishing insight. The Bábís, bereft of the counsels of Bahá'u'lláh, and sinking ever deeper into the mires of conflict and dissension, longed for His guidance, but knew not where to seek Him. No sooner did some of them hear of the Sage of Sulaymáníyyih, than they saw behind that veil the very Person of Bahá'u'lláh, and dispatched emissaries to find Him and implore His return. Bahá'u'lláh was surprised to see them, but He knew that He had to answer the call. This was the voice of God, the plan of Providence. Time had shown His indispensability to the community of the Báb.

On March 19th, 1856, Bahá'u'lláh returned to Bag͟hdád. His absence had lasted two years. Henceforth His power, His word, and His command were gladly welcomed by the Bábís. They had gone through a severe ordeal, and had learned their lesson in the school of adversity. No doubt opposition was still rife. Azal, a man of weak will, was held aloft by a handful of the ambitious and the self-seeking, as a puppet leader. But the Bábís had come to know them for what they were. Bahá'u'lláh exerted His utmost efforts to protect His half-brother from the seditious devices of plotters and agitators, but Azal was of an inferior type. He disregarded the sound advice of the One Who was his true friend, and became more and more implicated in vain scheming.

Hitherto, the believers in the Báb had been recruited from the Shí'ih sect of Islám. Now, under the ægis of Bahá'u'lláh, others came to enlist. He recreated the withered lives of the Bábís. They were told not to resist by violence any encroachments made on their liberties. In this manner He stemmed the tide of lawlessness that at one time had seriously menaced the integrity of the Bábí community. And so it came that Bahá'u'lláh's Divine guidance rallied the Bábís once again to a noble life. Once again they lived with faith in their hearts, their deeds testifying to the belief they bore.

During the years in Baghdád, Bahá'u'lláh revealed three of His best-known Writings: *The Hidden Words, The Seven Valleys,* and the *Kitáb-i-Íqán* or *The Book of Certitude.*

Walking on the banks of the Tigris, He reflected on the nearness of God, and the remoteness of Man, on the outpourings of God's Grace and Love, and Man's obstinate refusal to drink of that never-ending fountain. The result was *The Hidden Words,* written in a lucid and captivating prose, presenting those eternal verities that stand at the core of every revealed religion. Their sweeping range, the exquisite tenderness of their imagery and description, the majesty—the overwhelming majesty—of their conception, uplift the soul. In them the basic structure of religion is disclosed:

'This is that which hath descended from the realm of glory, uttered by the tongue of power and might, and revealed unto the Prophets of old. We have taken the inner essence thereof and clothed it in the garment of brevity, as a token of grace unto the righteous, that they may stand faithful unto the Covenant of God, may fulfil in their lives His trust, and in the realm of spirit obtain the gem of Divine virtue.'

'***O Son of Man!*** Veiled in My immemorial being and in the ancient eternity of My essence, I knew My love for thee; therefore I created thee, have engraved on thee Mine image and revealed to thee My beauty.'

'***O Son of Man!*** If thou lovest Me, turn away from thyself; and if thou seekest My pleasure, regard not thine own; that thou mayest die in Me and I may eternally live in thee.'

'***O Son of Being!*** With the hands of power I made thee and with the fingers of strength I created thee; and within thee have I placed the essence of My light. Be thou content with it and seek naught else, for My work is perfect and My command is binding. Question it not, nor have a doubt thereof.'

'***O Son of Man!*** Thou art My dominion and My dominion perisheth not, wherefore fearest thou thy perishing? Thou art My light and My light shall never be extinguished, why dost thou dread extinction? Thou art My glory and My glory fadeth not; thou art My robe and My robe shall never be outworn. Abide then in thy love for Me, that thou mayest find Me in the realm of glory.'

'***O Son of Spirit!*** Noble have I created thee, yet thou hast abased thyself. Rise then unto that for which thou wast created.'

'*O Companion of My Throne!* Hear no evil, and see no evil, abase not thyself, neither sigh and weep. Speak no evil, that thou mayest not hear it spoken unto thee, and magnify not the faults of others that thine own faults may not appear great; and wish not the abasement of anyone, that thine own abasement be not exposed. Live then the days of thy life, that are less than a fleeting moment, with thy mind stainless, thy heart unsullied, thy thoughts pure, and thy nature sanctified, so that, free and content, thou mayest put away this mortal frame, and repair unto the mystic paradise, and abide in the eternal kingdom for evermore.'

Such is the range of the counsel of *The Hidden Words*.

The Seven Valleys was composed in answer to a learned Ṣúfí. It is a gem of mystical prose matchless in its beauty, simplicity, and profundity. In this small book Bahá'u'lláh describes the stages that the seeker must needs traverse in his spiritual quest. The end of all search is to know God, and that knowledge can only be attained through His Manifestation. These seven valleys or stages are the Valleys of Search, Love, Knowledge, Unity, Contentment, Wonderment, True Poverty and Absolute Nothingness.

The Valley of Search

'In this valley the wayfarer rides the steed of patience. Without patience the wayfarer in this journey will reach nowhere and attain no goal. ... Were he to strive for ages, without beholding the beauty of the Friend, he should not become dejected ... In this journey the seeker reaches a stage wherein he finds all beings madly in search of the Friend. ...'

The Valley of Love

'In this valley the wayfarer rides the steed of pain; for without pain this journey will never end ... Every moment he would joyfully offer a hundred lives in the way of the Beloved and at every step he would throw a thousand heads in the path of the Friend ... Love admits of no life and seeks no existence. In death it sees life and in abasement seeks glory. ...'

The Valley of Knowledge

'In this valley the wayfarer, in his pure insight, finds no contradiction or difference in the creation of God. ... Many a knowledge he will find concealed in ignorance and hosts of wisdom manifest in knowledge. ...'

The Valley of Unity

'After traversing the Valley of Knowledge, which is the last plane of limitation, the wayfarer attains the first stage of the Valley of Unity whereupon he quaffs the chalice of abstraction and witnesses the Manifestations of Oneness. ... He hears with the ears of God and sees the mysteries of divine creation with the eyes of God. ... He will gaze upon all things with the eye of oneness and will find the Divine Sun, from the Heavenly Day-Spring, shedding the same light and splendour upon all beings and will see the lights of singleness reflected and visible upon all creation. ...'

The Valley of Contentment

'In this valley he will feel the breezes of divine contentment wafting from the plane of the spirit; he will burn the veils of want; and with inward and outward eyes, he will witness, within and without all things, the meaning of the verse: "In that Day, God will make all independent out of His abundance." His sorrow will be changed into joy, and his grief will be replaced by happiness; and his dejection and melancholy will yield to gladness and exultation. ...'

The Valley of Wonderment

'Now he sees the temple of wealth as want itself, and the essence of independence as sheer impotence. Now he is astonished by the beauty of the All-Glorious One, and now he wearies of his own existence. ... For, in this valley, the wayfarer is thrown into utter confusion. ... He witnesses a wondrous world and a new creation at every instant, and adds wonderment to wonderment; and he is astonished at the works of the Lord of Oneness. ...'

The Valley of True Poverty and Absolute Nothingness

'This state is that of dying from self and living in God, and being poor in self and becoming rich in the Desired One. ... And when you have attained this lofty plane and reached this mighty state, you will find the Friend and forget all else. ... In this city, even the veils of light vanish. ... Ecstasy alone can comprehend this theme, not discussion or argument. ...'

'The seven stages of this journey which have no visible end in the world of time, may be traversed by the detached wayfarer in seven steps, if not in seven breaths, nay in one breath—if, God willing, invisible assistance favour him....'

The *Kitáb-i-Íqán* or *The Book of Certitude* was written in answer to questions sent by an uncle of the Báb. In this book which the Guardian of the Bahá'í Faith has described as 'of unsurpassed pre-eminence among the writings of the Author of the Bahá'í Revelation,' Bahá'u'lláh offers a logical, illuminating and irrefutable explanation of the symbolism and the enigmatic texts of the Scriptures of the past, establishes the fact of progressive revelation, and adduces proofs to substantiate the divine mission of the Báb. Shoghi Effendi says furthermore, of *The Book of Certitude*, 'Well may it be claimed that of all the books revealed by the Author of the Bahá'í Revelation, this Book alone, by sweeping away the age-long barriers that have so insurmountably separated the great religions of the world, has laid down a broad and unassailable foundation for the complete and permanent reconciliation of their followers.'[9] No single quotation can adequately present a picture of the vast field covered by the contents of this momentous book. Speaking of the powers and the signs of God manifest in the entire realm of creation, Bahá'u'lláh says:

> '... Whatever is in the heavens and whatever is on the earth is a direct evidence of the revelation within it of the attributes and names of God, inasmuch as within every atom are enshrined the signs that bear eloquent testimony to the revelation of that most great Light. Methinks, but for the potency of that revelation, no being could ever exist. How resplendent the luminaries of knowledge that shine in an atom, and how vast the oceans of wisdom that surge within a drop! To a supreme degree is this true of man, who, among all created things, hath been invested with the robe of such gifts, and hath been singled out for the glory of such distinction. For in him are potentially revealed all the attributes and names of God to a degree that no other created being hath excelled or surpassed. All these names and attributes are applicable to him. Even as He hath said: "Man is My mystery, and I am his mystery". ... Man, the noblest and most perfect of all created things, excelleth them all in the intensity of this revelation, and is a fuller expression of its glory. And of all men, the most accomplished, the most distinguished and the most excellent are the Manifestations of the Sun of Truth. Nay, all else besides these Manifestations, live by the operation of their Will, and move and have their being through the outpourings of their grace. ... These Tabernacles of holiness, these primal Mirrors which reflect the light of unfading glory, are but expressions of Him Who is the Invisible of the Invisibles. By the revelation of these gems of divine virtue all the names and attributes of God, such as knowledge and power, sovereignty and dominion, mercy and wisdom, glory, bounty and grace, are made manifest.'[10]

The Manifestations of God, the Founders of the world's religions are the Bearers of God's will and purpose to mankind. They are the *logos*—the Word of God. In them nothing can be seen but the Reality and the Light of God.

> 'The door of the knowledge of the Ancient of Days being thus closed in the face of all beings, the Source of infinite grace ... hath caused those luminous Gems of Holiness to appear out of the realm of the spirit, in the noble form of the human temple, and be made manifest unto all men, that they may impart unto the world the mysteries of the unchangeable Being, and tell of the subtleties of His imperishable Essence. These sanctified Mirrors, these Day-springs of ancient glory are one and all the Exponents on earth of Him Who is the central Orb of the universe, its Essence and ultimate Purpose. From Him proceed their knowledge and power; from Him is derived their sovereignty. The beauty of their countenance is but a reflection of His image, and their revelation a sign of His deathless glory. They are the Treasuries of divine knowledge, and the Repositories of celestial wisdom. Through them is transmitted a grace that is infinite, and by them is revealed the light that can never fade.'[11]

This is only one aspect of the great theme that *The Book of Certitude* unfolds.

The Cause of the Báb was once more healthy and alive. The gloom of drift and anarchy had dispersed. From far and wide the Bábís came to bask in the sunshine of Bahá'u'lláh's love and guidance. Savants and learned men brought their intricate problems and received solutions to their satisfaction. But the renown attending upon the name of Bahá'u'lláh stirred anew the feelings of envy and hatred. A number of the Shí'ih divines assembled to determine a plan of action against the

Faith of the Báb and its revered Exponent. One should take note of the fact that Shaykh-i-Anṣárí, the most prominent of them all, refused to participate in their deliberations. They commissioned one of their members to wait upon Bahá'u'lláh and demand convincing proofs. This man did as he was bidden, and went back with a definite offer—Bahá'u'lláh would bring forth any proof that the clergy might require, on condition that they would on their part pledge themselves to accept His authority thereafter. Their emissary told them that he had witnessed nothing but truth and righteousness in the words and deeds of the Bábí Leader. Those men had come together, not to find truth, but to oppose it. Fearful lest Bahá'u'lláh should really bring forth the proof demanded by them, they refused to give any pledge, rejected the offer, and brought pressure upon the government of the Sháh to adopt repressive measures. The man who acted as their emissary, himself a noted cleric, was disgusted by their behaviour, and as long as he lived, told the people the truth of what actually transpired.

The Persian Consul in Baghdád supported the divines, and so insistent became their pleading, cajoling and finally intimidation that the Sháh took fright and instructed his envoy at Constantinople to enter into negotiations with the Turkish government. He wanted Bahá'u'lláh to be escorted to the frontier, and handed over to his men. Failing that he demanded the removal of Bahá'u'lláh to a locality far from the borders of Írán. Negotiations went on for sometime between the two States, and at last the Sulṭán ordered the Governor of Baghdád to send Bahá'u'lláh to Constantinople. His enemies were jubilant, and His friends horrified and sorrowful. Can we stretch our imagination far enough to visualise the despondency and the heart-ache of the Bábís in that month of April, 1863? Can we contemplate their grief?

Bahá'u'lláh moved to the garden of Riḍván, outside the gates of Baghdád. The Bábís thronged there to see the last of their Beloved so cruelly torn from their midst. It was the twenty-second day of April. With tears in their eyes they gathered around Him. He was calm, serene and unruffled. The hour had struck. To that company Bahá'u'lláh revealed Himself—He was the Promised One in Whose path the Báb had sacrificed His life, 'Him Whom God will make manifest', the Sháh-Bahrám, the Fifth Buddha, the Lord of Hosts, the Christ come in the station of the Father, the Master of the Day of Judgment.

> 'Canst thou discover any one but Me, O Pen, in this Day? What hath become of the creation and the manifestations thereof? What of the names and their kingdom? Whither are gone all created things, whether seen or unseen? What of the hidden secrets of the universe and its revelations? Lo, the entire creation hath passed away! Nothing remaineth except My Face, the Ever-Abiding, the Resplendent, the All-Glorious.
>
> 'This is the Day whereon naught can be seen except the splendours of the Light that shineth from the face of Thy Lord, the Gracious, the Most Bountiful. Verily, We have caused every soul to expire by virtue of Our irresistible and all-subduing sovereignty. We have, then, called into being a new creation, as a token of Our grace unto men. I am, verily, the All-Bountiful, the Ancient of Days.
>
> 'This is the Day whereon the unseen world crieth out: "Great is thy blessedness, O earth, for thou hast been made the foot-stool of thy God, and been chosen as the seat of His mighty throne." The realm of glory exclaimeth: "Would that my life could be sacrificed for thee, for He Who is the Beloved of the All-Merciful hath established His sovereignty upon thee, through the power of His Name that hath been promised unto all things, whether of the past or of the future ..."
>
> 'Arise, and proclaim unto the entire creation the tidings that He Who is the All-Merciful hath directed His steps towards the Riḍván and entered it. Guide, then, the

people unto the garden of delight which God hath made the Throne of His Paradise. ...

'Look not upon the creatures of God except with the eye of kindliness and of mercy, for Our loving providence hath pervaded all created things, and Our grace encompassed the earth and the heavens. This is the Day whereon the true servants of God partake of the life-giving waters of reunion, the Day whereon those that are nigh unto Him are able to drink of the soft-flowing river of immortality, and they who believe in His unity the wine of His Presence, through their recognition of Him Who is the Highest and Last End of all, in Whom the Tongue of Majesty and Glory voiceth the call: "The Kingdom is Mine. I, Myself, am, of Mine own right, its Ruler ..."

'Rejoice with exceeding gladness, O people of Bahá, as ye call to remembrance the Day of supreme felicity, the Day whereon the Tongue of the Ancient of Days hath spoken, as He departed from His House, proceeding to the Spot from which He shed upon the whole of creation the splendours of His name, the All-Merciful.'[12]

Heads were bent as the immensity of that Declaration touched the consciousness of men. Sadness had vanished; joy, celestial joy, prevailed.

Bahá'u'lláh left Baghdád on May 3rd, 1863, and arrived at the capital of the Turkish Empire three months later. He had been summoned there on the orders of the Sulṭán. Was He to face a formal trial? Was His case to be investigated by the Ottoman ruler in person? Was He to be led to prison in some distant part or to be kept indefinitely in Istanbul? Such questions undoubtedly assailed the minds of His people; no one was certain. Yet, although they could find no convincing answers, and although the future looked dark and perilous, many of His followers shared His exile with willing hearts.

From the Sublime Porte Bahá'u'lláh solicited no favour. His only protest was His silence. Several of the dignitaries of the capital called upon Him. Around an oriental court in the last century thrived malcontents and intriguers. While living in Baghdád, Bahá'u'lláh had been approached by a number of such persons who had hoped to win the affection of the Bábís. He had refused to meet them, and the few who gained admittance to His presence had received no encouragement. In Constantinople, Bahá'u'lláh adhered to the same rule. He refused all association with their designs. His Cause had not the remotest connection with sedition; in fact, the whole urge of His teachings was absolutely otherwise. Was this not also the path taken by Christ eighteen hundred years before? Calm, serene and patient, Bahá'u'lláh awaited the decision of His oppressors. Thus He spent four months at Istanbul. At last they banished Him to Adirnih (Adrianople).

So began another journey fraught with hardships. In falling snow, He and His companions set out towards their destination, without adequate means to provide against the rigours of a severe winter. The journey took them twelve days, and they arrived at Adirnih in a state of exhaustion. Yet even thus engulfed, Bahá'u'lláh could write in such terms as these: '*I am not impatient of calamities in His way, nor of afflictions for His love and at His good pleasure. ... Through affliction hath His light shone, and His praise been bright unceasingly; this has been His method through past ages and bygone times.*'

Bahá'u'lláh was now a prisoner of the Ottoman government. It had no charge to bring against Him, and yet it restrained the freedom of His movements.

At Adrianople Bahá'u'lláh issued an open and public announcement of His Revelation, and the Bábís, wherever they were, except for a few dissident voices, rallied to His Cause and submitted to His God-given Authority. Henceforth they were styled Bahá'ís. Azal, however, though outwardly subdued, was, with a number of the self-seeking around him, secretly engaged in opposition. The account of his intrigues and base dealings makes sorry reading. He and his accomplices dared not come into the open, because their motives were too transparent not to be detected and exposed. Azal imagined that he was undermining Bahá'u'lláh's position; in fact he was bringing ruin upon himself. Bahá'u'lláh did His utmost to save His brother, but His kindness and generosity met with more venom and hatred. Time, that unfaltering test of right and wrong, eventually showed the hollowness of Azal's contention and the misery of his purpose. He introduced poison into Bahá'u'lláh's food. Bahá'u'lláh's life was saved, but the effects of that deadly substance remained with Him to the end of His days. Having failed in his dastardly attempt, Azal turned round and pointed an accusing finger at Bahá'u'lláh. It was his Brother, he alleged, Who had poisoned the food, and then accidentally partaken of it. To-day, at the remove of a century, we can pity the malefactor, and feel amused by his calumnies and presumptions. At the time, such vile conduct served to increase the rigours of Bahá'u'lláh's life.

The following is an extract from the autobiography of Ustád Muhammad-'Alí, the barber attendant upon Bahá'u'lláh in Adrianople:

> One day, while I was attending at the bath, waiting for the Blessed Perfection to arrive, Azal came in, washed himself and began to apply henna. I sat down to serve him and he began to talk to me. He mentioned a former Governor of Nayríz who had killed the believers and had been an inveterate enemy of the Cause. Azal went on to praise courage and bravery and said that some were brave by nature and at the right time it showed in their conduct. He again mentioned Nayríz and said that at one time there was left of the children of the believers only one boy, of

ten or eleven years. One day, when the Governor was in the bath, this boy went in with a knife, and as the Governor came out of the water, he stabbed him in the belly and ripped him open. The Governor cried out and his servants rushed into the bath, saw the boy with the knife in his hand and attacked him. Then they went to see how their master was, and the boy, although wounded, rose up and stabbed him again. Azal again began to praise bravery and to say how wonderful it is to be courageous. He then said, 'See what they are doing in the Cause; everybody has risen up against me, even my brother, and in my wretched state I know nothing of comfort.' His tone and implication were that he, being the successor of the Báb, was the wronged one and his Brother an usurper and aggressor. (I take refuge in God!) Then he again said that bravery is praiseworthy, and the Cause of God needs help. In all this talk, relating the story of the Governor of Nayríz and praising bravery and encouraging me, he was really urging me to kill Bahá'u'lláh.

The effect of all this upon me was so disturbing that I had never felt so shattered in my life. I felt as if the building were tumbling about me. I said nothing, but in a very agitated state of mind went out to the ante-room and sat upon the bench there. I told myself that I would go back to the bath and cut off his head, no matter what the consequences. Then I reflected that to kill him was not an easy matter and perhaps I would offend Bahá'u'lláh. Suppose I kill this man, I said to myself, and then go into the presence of the Blessed Perfection and He asks me why I killed him, what answer could I give? This thought prevented me from carrying out my intention. I returned to the bath and being very angry told Azal to 'clear off'.* Azal began to whimper and to tremble and asked me to pour water over his head to wash off the henna. I complied and he washed and went out of the bath in a state of great trepidation and I have never seen him since.

My condition was such that nothing could calm me. As it happened the Blessed Perfection did not come to the bath that day, but Mírzá Músá (Bahá'u'lláh's faithful

* In Persian this is highly insulting.

brother) came, and I told him that Azal had set me on fire with his fearful suggestion. Mírzá Músá said, 'He has been thinking of this for years; take no notice of him. He has always been thinking in this way.' No one else came to the bath so I closed it. I then went to the Master* and told Him that Mírzá Yaḥyá had spoken words which had infuriated me and that I had wanted to kill him but did not. The Master said this was something which people did not realise and told me not to speak of it but to keep it secret. I then went to Mírzá Áqá Ján (Bahá'u'lláh's amanuensis and secretary) and reported the whole incident to him and asked him to tell Bahá'u'lláh. Áqá Ján returned and said: 'Bahá'u'lláh says to tell Ustád Muḥammad-'Alí not to mention this to anyone.'

That night I collected all the writings of Azal and went to the coffee room of Bahá'u'lláh's house and burnt them in the brazier. Before doing so I showed them to seven or eight of the believers present, saying 'These are the writings of Azal'. They all protested and asked me why I did it. I answered that until to-day I esteemed Azal highly, but now he was less than a dog in my sight.

From Adrianople, and later from 'Akká, Bahá'u'lláh addressed the rulers of the world in a series of Letters. To them He declared His Divine Mission, and called them to serve peace, justice and righteousness. The majestic sweep of His counsel and admonition revealed in these letters, arrests the deepest attention of every earnest student of the Bahá'í Faith.

Here we see a Prisoner wronged by the world, judged and condemned by a conspiracy of tyrants, facing the concourse of sovereigns, nay, the generality of mankind. He stands in judgment upon the values of human society, and undaunted, He throws a bold challenge, not alone to His oppressors, not alone to ephemeral shadows of earthly might and dominion, but principally to those dark passions and motives which dare to intervene between man and the goal destined for him by

* 'Abdu'l-Bahá, Bahá'u'lláh's son and appointed successor.

his Maker. Here, an Exile rejected and betrayed is seen to be the True and Only Judge.

One of the rulers to receive a Letter from Bahá'u'lláh was Náṣiri'd-Dín, the Sháh of Persia, the sovereign at whose bidding Bahá'u'lláh had been exiled from His native land, at whose instance the Ottoman government had called Him away from 'Iráq. Náṣiri'd-Dín Sháh was a capricious, overbearing tyrant who was confident that the removal of Bahá'u'lláh from the vicinity of his realms to far-away Roumelia was a master-stroke against the fortunes of the Faith which he abhorred. And now there was delivered into his hands a letter from the same Exile, vibrant with a power beyond his grasp:

> 'I have seen, O Sháh, in the path of God what eye hath not seen nor ear heard. ... How numerous the tribulations which have rained, and will soon rain upon Me! I advance with My face set towards Him Who is the Almighty, the All-Bounteous, whilst behind Me glideth the serpent. Mine eyes have rained down tears until My bed is drenched. I sorrow not for Myself, however. By God! Mine head yearneth for the spear out of love of its Lord. I never passed a tree, but Mine heart addressed it saying: "O would that thou wert cut down in My name, and My body crucified upon thee, in the path of My Lord!" ... By God! Though weariness lay Me low, and hunger consume Me, and the bare rock be My bed, and My fellows the beasts of the field, I will not complain, but will endure patiently as those endued with constancy and firmness have endured patiently, through the power of God, the Eternal King and Creator of the nations, and will render thanks unto God under all conditions. We pray that, out of His bounty—exalted be He—He may release, through this imprisonment, the necks of men from chains and fetters, and cause them to turn, with sincere faces, towards His Face, Who is the Mighty, the Bounteous. Ready is He to answer whosoever calleth upon Him, and nigh is He unto such as commune with Him.'[13]

The messenger who took Bahá'u'lláh's Letter to the Sháh was tortured and put to death. He was a young man only seventeen years old, Áqá Buzurg of Khurásán whom Bahá'í history knows as Badí' (the Wonderful). At one time he was the despair of his family. But a day came when he felt that he had to seek Bahá'u'lláh and obtain new life from His hands. It was an immense distance from Khurásán, the north-eastern province of Persia, to the shores of the Mediterranean Sea. Unflinchingly he set forth on foot and took the hazardous road to the abode of his Lord. Bahá'u'lláh had revealed the Tablet to the Sháh at Adrianople, and now He was in the prison barracks of 'Akká. Many vied for the honour to be the bearer of that Letter. But Bahá'u'lláh waited. When the young man from Khurásán arrived and gained admittance into the prison, Bahá'u'lláh said that the one who was to take His Tablet to the Sháh had come. Badí' travelled back to Persia in the manner he came. As bidden by Bahá'u'lláh, he sought no one's company, but alone made his way to Ṭihrán. It took him four months. Reaching the capital, he made ready for his final act. He fasted and kept watch, and the moment he encountered the Sháh outside the capital, he called out, 'O King! I have come to thee from Sheba with a weighty message.' The monarch knew by that ardour and zeal whose messenger this young man was. Badí' was immediately put under arrest and tortured to reveal the names of his associates. He bore all his sufferings with fortitude. Then they pounded his head with the butt of a rifle, and threw his body into a pit*

But the call of Bahá'u'lláh, in that Tablet to the Sháh, resounds throughout the years:

> 'O King! I was but a man like others, asleep upon My couch, when lo, the breezes of the All-Glorious were wafted over Me, and taught Me the knowledge of all that hath been. This thing is not from Me, but from One Who

* See page 79.

is Almighty and All-Knowing. And He bade Me lift up My voice between earth and heaven, and for this there befell Me what hath caused the tears of every man of understanding to flow. The learning current amongst men I studied not; their schools I entered not. Ask of the city wherein I dwelt, that thou mayest be well assured that I am not of them who speak falsely. This is but a leaf which the winds of the will of Thy Lord, the Almighty, the All-Praised, have stirred. Can it be still when the tempestuous winds are blowing? Nay, by Him Who is the Lord of all Names and Attributes! They move it as they list.'[14]

At a later period Bahá'u'lláh addressed the town of His birth, Ṭihrán, with these pregnant words:

'Rejoice with great joy, for God hath made thee "the Dayspring of His light", inasmuch as within thee was born the Manifestation of His Glory. Be thou glad for this name that hath been conferred upon thee—a name through which the Day Star of grace hath shed its splendour, through which both earth and heaven have been illumined.

'Ere long will the state of affairs within thee be changed, and the reins of power fall into the hands of the people. Verily, thy Lord is the All-Knowing. His authority embraceth all things. Rest thou assured in the gracious favour of thy Lord. The eye of His loving-kindness shall everlastingly be directed towards thee.'[15]

To Sulṭán 'Abdu'l-'Azíz, the Ottoman ruler who ordered His exile, Bahá'u'lláh spoke in such tones of authority:

'Hearken, O King, to the speech of Him that speaketh the truth, Him that doth not ask thee to recompense Him with the things God hath chosen to bestow upon thee, Him Who unerringly treadeth the straight Path. He it is Who summoneth thee unto God, thy Lord, Who showeth thee the right course, the way that leadeth to true felicity, that haply thou mayest be of them with whom it shall be well. ...

'Overstep not the bounds of moderation, and deal justly with them that serve thee. Bestow upon them according to their needs, and not to the extent that will enable them to lay up riches for themselves, to deck their persons, to embellish their homes, to acquire the things that are of no benefit unto them, and to be numbered with the extravagant. Deal with them with undeviating justice, so that none among them may either suffer want, or be pampered with luxuries. This is but manifest justice.

'Allow not the abject to rule over and dominate them who are noble and worthy of honour, and suffer not the high-minded to be at the mercy of the contemptible and worthless, for this is what We observed upon Our arrival in the City (Constantinople), and to it We bear witness. We found among its inhabitants some who were possessed of an affluent fortune and lived in the midst of excessive riches, whilst others were in dire want and abject poverty. This ill beseemeth thy sovereignty, and is unworthy of thy rank. ... Strive thou to rule with equity among men, that God may exalt thy name and spread abroad the fame of thy justice in all the world.'[16]

He foresaw the catastrophes which would overtake the Ottoman domains in the wake of an unregenerate policy:

'The course of things shall be altered, and conditions shall wax so grievous, that the very sands on the desolate hills will moan, and the trees on the mountains will weep, and blood will flow out of all things. Then wilt thou behold the people in sore distress.'[17]

Napoleon III, the French Emperor, gave the Letter sent to him a reception far from courteous. He is quoted as saying with overweening arrogance, 'If this man is God, I am two gods.' Then a second Tablet was sent to him from the prison of 'Akká:

'It is not Our wish to address thee words of condemnation, out of regard for the dignity We conferred upon thee in this mortal life. We, verily, have chosen courtesy, and made it the true mark of such as are nigh unto Him. Courtesy is, in truth, a raiment which fitteth all men, whether young or old. ... For what thou hast done, thy kingdom shall be thrown into confusion, and thine empire shall pass from thine hands, as a punishment for that which thou hast wrought. Then wilt thou know how thou hast plainly erred. Commotions shall seize all the people in that land, unless thou arisest to help this Cause, and followest Him Who is the Spirit of God (Jesus Christ) in this, the Straight Path. Hath thy pomp made thee proud? By My Life! It shall not endure; nay, it shall soon pass away, unless thou holdest fast by this firm Cord. We see abasement hastening after thee, whilst thou art of the heedless. It behooveth thee when thou hearest His Voice calling from the seat of glory to cast away all that thou possessest, and cry out: "Here am I, O Lord of all that is in heaven and all that is on earth." '[18]

In the same Tablet Bahá'u'lláh told the French Emperor:

> 'O King of Paris! Tell the priests to ring the bells no longer. By God, the True One! The Most Mighty Bell hath appeared in the form of Him Who is the Most Great Name, and the fingers of the will of thy Lord, the Most Exalted, the Most High, toll it out in the heaven of Immortality, in His Name, the All-Glorious.'

This Tablet was sent in 1869. Barely a year later, Napoleon suffered defeat. The French agent in 'Akká who had translated Bahá'u'lláh's Tablet into French and had sent it to the Emperor, noticing the swift descent of doom upon the throne of that monarch, accepted the Faith of Bahá'u'lláh.

William I, the German Emperor, was warned to take heed of the fate of the ruler overthrown by the triumph of his arms:

> 'Do thou remember the one whose power transcended thy power, and whose station excelled thy station. Where is he? Whither are gone the things he possessed? Take warning, and be not of them that are fast asleep. He it was who cast the Tablet of God behind him, when We made

known unto him what the hosts of tyranny had caused Us to suffer. Wherefore, disgrace assailed him from all sides, and he went down to dust in great loss. Think deeply, O King, concerning him, and concerning them who, like unto thee, have conquered cities and ruled over men. The All-Merciful brought them down from their palaces to their graves. Be warned, be of them who reflect.'[19]

Bahá'u'lláh also prophesied the ordeals of the German Empire:

'O banks of the Rhine! We have seen you covered with gore, inasmuch as the swords of retribution were drawn against you; and you shall have another turn. And We hear the lamentations of Berlin, though she be today in conspicuous glory.'[20]

The Tablet to Pope Pius IX is of particular interest and concern to the Christian world. To the Supreme Pontiff at Rome, Bahá'u'lláh wrote:

'O Pope! Rend the veils asunder. He Who is the Lord of Lords is come overshadowed with clouds, and the decree hath been fulfilled by God, the Almighty, the Unrestrained. ... He, verily, hath again come down from Heaven even as He came down from it the first time. Beware that thou dispute not with Him even as the Pharisees disputed with Him (Jesus) without a clear token or proof. ... Leave thou the world behind thee, and turn towards thy Lord, through Whom the whole earth hath been illumined. ... Dwellest thou in palaces whilst He Who is the King of Revelation liveth in the most desolate of abodes? ... Arise in the name of thy Lord, the God of Mercy, amidst the peoples of the earth, and seize thou the Cup of Life with the hands of confidence, and first drink thou therefrom, and proffer it then to such as turn towards it amongst the peoples of all faiths. ...

'Call thou to remembrance Him Who was the Spirit (Jesus), Who, when He came, the most learned of His age pronounced judgment against Him in His own country, whilst he who was only a fisherman believed in Him. ... Consider those who opposed the Son (Jesus), when He came unto them with sovereignty and power. How many the Pharisees who were waiting to behold Him, and were lamenting over their separation from Him! And yet, when the fragrance of His coming was wafted over them, and His beauty was unveiled, they turned aside from Him and disputed with Him. ... None save a very few, who were destitute of any power amongst men, turned towards His face. And yet, today, every man endowed with power and invested with sovereignty prideth himself on His Name! In like manner, consider how numerous, in these days, are the monks who, in My Name, have secluded themselves in their churches, and who, when the appointed time was fulfilled, and We unveiled Our beauty, knew Us not, though they call upon Me at eventide and at dawn. ...

'The Word which the Son concealed is made manifest. It hath been sent down in the form of the human temple in this day. Blessed be the Lord Who is the Father! He, verily, is come unto the nations in His most great majesty. Turn your faces towards Him, O concourse of the righteous! ... This is the day whereon the Rock (Peter) crieth out and shouteth, and celebrateth the praise of its Lord, the All-Possessing, the Most High, saying: "Lo! The Father is come, and that which ye were promised in the Kingdom is fulfilled! ... " My body longeth for the cross, and Mine head waiteth the thrust of the spear, in the path of the All-Merciful, that the world may be purged from its transgressions. ...'[21]

Alexander II of Russia was another of the sovereign heads of the world who received a Tablet from Bahá'u'lláh:

'O Czar of Russia! Incline thine ear unto the voice of God, the King, the Holy, and turn thou unto Paradise, the Spot wherein abideth He Who, among the Concourse on high, beareth the most excellent titles, and Who, in the kingdom of creation, is called by the name of God, the Effulgent, the All-Glorious. Beware lest thy desire deter thee from turning towards the face of thy Lord, the

Compassionate, the Most Merciful. ... Whilst I lay chained and fettered in the prison, one of thy ministers extended Me his aid. Wherefore hath God ordained for thee a station which the knowledge of none can comprehend except His knowledge. Beware lest thou barter away this sublime station. ... Beware lest thy sovereignty withold thee from Him Who is the Supreme Sovereign. ...

'Hearken unto My Voice that calleth from My prison, that it may acquaint thee with the things that have befallen My Beauty, at the hands of them that are the manifestations of My glory, and that thou mayest perceive how great hath been My patience, notwithstanding My might, and how immense My forbearance, notwithstanding My power. By My Life! Couldst thou but know the things sent down by My Pen, and discover the treasures of My Cause, and the pearls of My mysteries which lie hid in the seas of My names and in the goblets of My words, thou wouldst, in thy love for My Name, and in thy longing for My glorious and sublime Kingdom, lay down thy life in My path. Know thou that though My body be beneath the swords of My foes, and My limbs be beset with incalculable afflictions, yet My spirit is filled with a gladness with which all the joys of the earth can never compare.

'... I, verily, have not sought to extol Mine Own Self, but rather God Himself were ye to judge fairly. Naught can be seen in Me except God and His Cause, could ye but perceive it. I am the One Whom the tongue of Isaiah hath extolled, the One with Whose Name both the Torah and the Evangel were adorned.'[22]

In the *Kitáb-i-Aqdas* (*The Most Holy Book*), Emperor Francis Joseph of Austria is reminded of his journey to the Holy Land:

'O Emperor of Austria! He Who is the Dayspring of God's Light dwelt in the prison of 'Akká, at the time when thou didst set forth to visit the Aqṣá Mosque (Jerusalem). Thou passed Him by, and inquired not about Him, by Whom every house is exalted, and every lofty gate unlocked. We, verily, made it (Jerusalem) a place whereunto the world should turn, that they might remember Me, and yet thou hast rejected Him Who is the Object of this remembrance, when He appeared with the Kingdom of God, thy Lord and the Lord of the worlds. We have been with thee at all times, and found thee clinging unto the Branch and heedless of the Root. Thy Lord, verily, is a witness unto what I say. We grieved to see thee circle round Our Name, whilst unaware of Us, though We were before thy face. Open thine eyes, that thou mayest behold this glorious Vision, and recognize Him Whom thou invokest in the daytime and in the night-season, and gaze on the Light that shineth above this luminous Horizon.'[23]

In the same Book, Bahá'u'lláh issues a call to the American Continent:

'O Rulers of America and the Presidents of the Republics therein! Hearken to the strains of the Dove, on the branch of eternity, singing the melody: "There is no God but Me, the Everlasting, the Forgiver, the Generous." Adorn the temple of dominion with the ornament of justice and the fear of God, and its head with the crown of remembrance of your Lord. ... The Promised One has appeared in this exalted station, whereat all creation, both seen and unseen, smiled and rejoiced. ... Bind with the hands of justice the broken, and crush the oppressor with the rod of the commandments of your Lord, the Ordainer, the All-Wise.'[24]

The Tablet to Queen Victoria epitomizes the Message lying at the core of His Letters to the sovereigns of the world. Those—and legions they are—who are baffled and bewildered by the ferocity of present-day political strife and international discord, cannot afford to overlook this momentous document. To them it brings the answer which they seek in vain elsewhere:

'O Queen in London! Incline thine ear unto the voice of thy Lord, the Lord of all mankind, calling from the Divine Lote-Tree: Verily, no God is there but Me, the Almighty, the All-Wise! Cast away all that is on earth, and attire the head of thy kingdom with the crown of the remembrance of thy Lord, the All-Glorious. He, in truth, hath come unto the world in His most great glory, and all that hath been mentioned in the Gospel hath been fulfilled. ...

'Lay aside thy desire, and set then thy heart towards thy Lord, the Ancient of Days. We make mention of thee for the sake of God, and desire that thy name may be exalted through thy remembrance of God, the Creator of earth and heaven. He, verily, is witness unto that which I say. We have been informed that thou hast forbidden the trading in slaves, both men and women. This, verily, is what God hath enjoined in this wondrous Revelation. God hath, truly, destined a reward for thee, because of this ...

'We have also heard that thou hast entrusted the reins of counsel into the hands of the representatives of the people. Thou, indeed, hast done well, for thereby the foundations of the edifice of thine affairs will be strengthened, and the hearts of all that are beneath thy shadow, whether high or low, will be tranquillized. It behoveth them, however, to be trustworthy among His servants, and to regard themselves as the representatives of all that dwell on earth. ... Blessed is he that entereth the assembly for the sake of God, and judgeth between men with pure justice. He, indeed, is of the blissful.[25]

... 'O ye the elected representatives of the people in every land! Take ye counsel together, and let your concern be only for that which profiteth mankind, and bettereth the condition thereof, if ye be of them that scan heedfully. Regard the world as the human body which, though at its creation whole and perfect, hath been afflicted, through various causes, with grave disorders and maladies. Not for one day did it gain ease, nay, its sickness waxed more severe, as it fell under the treatment of ignorant physicians, who gave full rein to their personal desires, and have erred grievously. And if, at one time, through the care of an able physician, a member of that body was healed, the rest remained afflicted as before. Thus informeth you the All-Knowing, the All-Wise.

'We behold it, in this day, at the mercy of rulers so drunk with pride that they cannot discern clearly their own best advantage, much less recognize a Revelation so bewildering and challenging as this. And whenever any one of them hath striven to improve its condition, his motive hath been his own gain, whether confessedly so or not; and the unworthiness of this motive hath limited his power to heal or cure.

'That which the Lord hath ordained as the sovereign remedy and mightiest instrument for the healing of all the world is the union of all its peoples in one universal Cause, one common Faith. This can in no wise be achieved except through the power of a skilled, an all-powerful and inspired Physician. This, verily, is the truth, and all else naught but error. Each time that Most Mighty Instrument hath come, and that Light shone forth from the Ancient Dayspring, He was withheld by ignorant physicians who, even as clouds, interposed themselves between Him and the world.'[26]

After this clear analysis of the causes of unrest and affliction, Bahá'u'lláh speaks of the attempts made to frustrate His Divinely-ordained task of regenerating the world, points to the ever-mounting burden of armaments, and still addressing the concourse of the rulers and the sovereigns of the earth, He pleads the cause of the people and the victims of injustice:

'Thus We unfold to your eyes that which profiteth you, if ye but perceive. Your people are your treasures. Beware lest your rule violate the commandments of God, and ye deliver your wards to the hands of the robber. By them ye rule, by their means ye subsist, by their aid ye conquer. Yet, how disdainfully ye look upon them! How strange, how very strange.'[27]

And then Bahá'u'lláh gives a final and a severe warning to those who wield authority amongst men:

'Now that ye have refused the Most Great Peace, hold ye fast unto this, the Lesser Peace, that haply ye may in some degree better your own condition and that of your dependents.

'O rulers of the earth! Be reconciled amongst yourselves, that ye may need no more armaments save in a measure to safeguard your territories and dominions. Beware lest ye disregard the counsel of the All-Knowing, the Faithful.

'Be united, O kings of the earth, for thereby will the tempest of discord be stilled amongst you, and your people find rest, if ye be of them that comprehend. Should any one among you take up arms against another, rise ye all against him, for this is naught but manifest justice.'[28]

This is collective security, so hotly debated, so unnecessarily complicated, and so ill served in the period between Bahá'u'lláh's declaration and the two world conflagrations. Bahá'u'lláh states the case of collective security very plainly and very simply. He makes it synonymous with justice. And of justice, He says in *The Hidden Words*:

'O Son of Spirit! The best beloved of all things in My sight is justice; turn not away therefrom if thou desirest Me, and neglect it not that I may confide in thee. By its aid thou shalt see with thine own eyes and not through the eyes of others, and shalt know of thine own knowledge and not through the knowledge of thy neighbour. Ponder this in thy heart; how it behoveth thee to be. Verily justice is My gift to thee and the sign of My loving-kindness. Set it then before thine eyes.'[29]

It is related that Queen Victoria's comment on reading Bahá'u'lláh's Tablet was: 'If this is of God, it will endure; if not, it can do no harm.'

Bahá'u'lláh's fame was now spreading far and wide. Except for a very small number who supported Azal, the Bábís, wherever they were, had accepted the Divine mandate of

Bahá'u'lláh. The Turkish authorities in Adrianople treated Him with great courtesy and marked respect. Governors such as Sulaymán Páshá and Khurshíd Páshá sought His company with eagerness. And many of His followers from Persia and neighbouring lands travelled to Adrianople to drink deeply at the fount of His Revelation. All these things stung his adversaries to fresh action. Azal and his miserable accomplices, discredited and disowned by the community, their tortuous devices and designs abortive and exposed, having failed repeatedly to shake the allegiance which the Bábís had given to Bahá'u'lláh, next tried to poison the minds of the rulers of the Ottoman Empire against Him—their true Benefactor Whom they hated so venomously. They sent anonymous letters to Constantinople, in which they accused Bahá'u'lláh of collusion with the Bulgarian leaders and European powers in a plot to capture the capital with the aid of His followers. Sulṭán 'Abdu'l-'Azíz and his ministers took fright and Azal's treachery bore him bitter fruit, for not only were Bahá'u'lláh and His people condemned to imprisonment in the desolate barracks of 'Akká, but Azal himself was banished, to Cyprus—to oblivion. He outlived Bahá'u'lláh, dragging on existence until the year 1912, impenitent to the end, a broken man, the victim of his passions and selfish pursuits.

One morning, without any previous intimation, soldiers were posted round the house of Bahá'u'lláh, and His followers were told to prepare for their departure from Adrianople. Bahá'u'lláh writes thus of that event:

'The loved ones of God and His kindred were left on the first night without food. ... The people surrounded the house, and Muslims and Christians wept over Us. ... We perceived that the weeping of the people of the Son (Christians) exceeded the weeping of others—a sign for such as ponder.'[30]

Áqá Riḍá, a steadfast follower of Bahá'u'lláh, who shared His exiles from Baghdád to 'Akká, relates that, 'A great tumult seized the people. All were perplexed and full of regret. ... Some expressed their sympathy, others consoled us and wept over us. ... Most of our possessions were auctioned at half their value.'[31]

Some of the foreign consuls resident in Adrianople offered their assistance to Bahá'u'lláh, which He courteously refused. The Governor, Khurshíd Páshá, considered his government's decision a travesty of justice, and felt unable to carry it through. He deputed another official to inform Bahá'u'lláh of the judgment passed upon Him. People thronged to bid farewell to the One Whom they had learned to love and esteem. With tears welling from their eyes, they kissed the hem of His robe.

On August 12th, 1868, Bahá'u'lláh and His family, accompanied by a Turkish escort, took once again the road to exile. They reached 'Akká on the last day of the month.

'Akká, Ptolemais of the ancient world, St. Jean d'Acre of the Crusaders that defied the siege of Richard I of England, and in a later age refused to bow to the might of Napoleon, a city that had gathered renown throughout the centuries, had indeed fallen into disrepute at this period of its chequered history. Its air and water were foul and pestilential. Proverb had it that a bird flying over 'Akká would fall dead. To its forbidding barracks were consigned the desperadoes and dangerous criminals of the Ottoman realms—there to perish.

This was also the city of which David had spoken as 'The Strong City', which Hosea had called 'A door of hope', of which Ezekiel had said, 'Afterward he brought me to the gate, even the gate that looketh toward the east: And, behold, the glory of the God of Israel came from the way of the east: and his voice was like a noise of many waters: and the earth shined with his glory. ... And the glory of the Lord came into the house by the way of the gate whose prospect is toward the east.'[32] And the Founder of Islám had thus eulogised this very city, '*Blessed the man that hath visited 'Akká, and blessed be he that hath visited the visitor of 'Akká. ... He that raiseth therein the call to prayer, his voice will be lifted up unto Paradise.*'[33]

The 'Akká which opened its gates to receive as a prisoner the Deliverer of the world, was a city that had fathomed the depths of misery. And Bahá'u'lláh's exile to Palestine, the Holy Land, His incarceration in the grim citadel of 'Akká, was intended by His adversaries to be the final blow which, in their calculations, would shatter His Faith and fortune. How significant and momentous will this exile seem, if we recall certain prophecies uttered in the past. 'Abdu'l-Bahá, the Son of Bahá'u'lláh and the Expounder of His Message, thus speaks of this stupendous event:

> 'When Bahá'u'lláh came to this prison in the Holy Land, the wise men realized that the glad tidings which God gave through the tongue of the Prophets two or three thousand years before, were again manifested, and that God was faithful to His promise; for to some of the Prophets He had revealed and given the good news that "The Lord of Hosts should be manifested in the Holy Land." All these promises were fulfilled; and it is difficult to understand how Bahá'u'lláh could have been obliged to leave Persia, and to pitch His tent in this Holy Land, but for the persecution of His enemies, His banishment and exile.'[34]

'Lift up your heads, O ye gates,' David had so majestically announced; 'even lift them up, ye everlasting doors; and the King of glory shall come in. Who is this King of glory? The Lord of hosts, he is the King of glory.'[35]

'The wilderness and the solitary place shall be glad for them,' Isaiah had said, 'and the desert shall rejoice, and blossom as the rose. It shall blossom abundantly, and rejoice even with joy and singing: the glory of Lebanon shall be given unto it, the excellency of Carmel and Sharon; they shall see the glory of the Lord, and the excellency of our God.'[36]

'The Lord will roar from Zion,' had been Amos's testimony, 'and utter his voice from Jerusalem; and the habitations of the shepherds shall mourn, and the top of Carmel shall wither.'[37]

And Micah had thus foreseen, '... from Assyria, and from the fortified cities, and from the fortress even to the river, and from sea to sea, and from mountain to mountain', he shall come.[38]

Life in the barracks of 'Akká was indeed hard and hazardous. The prisoners were about seventy in number: men, women and children, all huddled in a few dirty and meagrely protected cells. They were viewed with the utmost hostility by the townsmen. On their arrival they were greeted derisively at the landing-place by a group of idle onlookers who had gathered in a mocking mood to see the 'God of the Persians'. The first night in the prison they were, Bahá'u'lláh tells us, '*deprived of either food or drink. ... They even begged for water and were refused*'. Their rations consisted of three flat loaves of black and unpalatable bread for each person. Later slight concessions were made, but food remained pitiably inadequate and the water supply was polluted. Before long disease raged among them. In vain they pleaded with the governor for medical succour. All but two were ill and helpless. Three of them died. Two of these were brothers who died, in the words of Bahá'u'lláh, '*locked in each other's arms*'. Their bodies could not be removed, because the guards required money to induce them to carry out their duty. Bahá'u'lláh gave the carpet on which He slept, to be sold for this purpose. The sum thus raised was given to the wardens, and even then the dead were not given a proper burial. But amidst their afflictions, the prisoners retained their serenity. They were happy because they were co-sharers in the sufferings of their Lord, and dwelt near His Person.

For a long while the Bahá'ís in Írán and elsewhere possessed no news of Bahá'u'lláh. Later it was possible to establish communications, and a number came to 'Akká to find prison walls intervening between them and the One Whose presence they so eagerly sought. Some had journeyed on foot over the high mountains of Western Írán and the burning deserts of 'Iráq and Syria. They had perforce to content themselves with a momentary glimpse of His figure, as He stood behind the bars, and they beyond the second of the moats which surrounded the prison. Only a wave of His hands from afar was their reward; and then they turned homewards, grateful for the bounty conferred upon them. That was enough to kindle a more vigorous flame in their hearts, enough to make their dedication more dedicated. Others came in their wake, and took back the memory of that Figure appearing at the window, behind iron bars—a memory which they treasured above everything in their lives. And some had the supreme bounty of gaining admittance to the 'Most Great Prison', to the Presence of Bahá'u'lláh.

Close confinement in the barracks lasted until October, 1870. Military reinforcements had been sent to that part of the Ottoman Empire and the citadel of 'Akká was in demand for their accommodation. The prisoners were led out, but not to freedom. Bahá'u'lláh and His family were conducted to a small house within the city walls, and others were lodged in a caravanserai. They were still held as prisoners inside the town.

Four months before this event a further tragedy, dire and poignant, had cast its shadow upon them. That was the death of Mírzá Mihdí, entitled 'The Purest Branch', a younger son of Bahá'u'lláh. He had shared his Father's exile from childhood, and was His amanuensis. One day at dusk, while walking on the roof of the prison, engaged in his devotions, he fell through a skylight and received fatal injuries. 'His dying supplication to a grieving Father,' writes Shoghi Effendi, the Guardian of the Faith, 'was that his life might be accepted as a ransom for those who were prevented from attaining the presence of their Beloved.' He was twenty-two years old.

One might imagine that release from strict bondage would have spelt relief. Such was not the case however. Enclosed within the barracks, Bahá'u'lláh and His companions had few contacts with the inhabitants of 'Akká, while rumours of the ugliest kind regarding them were spread abroad. Ignorant of the real identity of Bahá'u'lláh, the townsmen relegated Him and His followers to the same category as the previous inmates of the prison of 'Akká. Even worse, in their unrestrained imaginations, they laid every odious act to the charge of the Bahá'ís, whom they described as renegades from the true faith, traitors to the august person of the Sulṭán, plotters against the peace and the security of the land, licentious ruffians and outlaws who deserved the censure of the righteous. These were the same views held of Christians in the first centuries of the Christian Era. The Bahá'ís were ushered into this charged atmosphere of undisguised hatred and contempt. Their task of conciliation was indeed herculean.

Then happened an awful act, committed by seven of the Bahá'ís, which added to the furies of the populace. When the Ottoman authorities sent Bahá'u'lláh to the prison of 'Akká, they included in the band of His followers accompanying Him, some of the accomplices of Azal, as spies. These men never lost an opportunity to torment the exiles and spread falsehoods. Their constant schemings brought fresh sorrows in their wake, further incited the townsmen against Bahá'u'lláh, and placed His life in great jeopardy. On His part Bahá'u'lláh repeatedly exhorted His followers to forbearance, and counselled them to avoid any deed which bore, no matter how remotely, any resemblance to retaliation. But the treachery and malevolence of the adversaries waxed high. Then it was that seven of the Bahá'ís chose to disregard the injunctions of Bahá'u'lláh, and slew three of the evil men. This flagrant act not only aroused the people, but forcing the intervention of the officials, subjected the Person of Bahá'u'lláh to arrest and interrogation. 'Abdu'l-Bahá was put in chains for one night. Viewing this calamitous event, Bahá'u'lláh wrote: '*My captivity cannot harm Me. That which can harm Me is the conduct of those who love Me, who claim to be related to Me, and yet perpetrate what causeth My heart and My pen to groan. My captivity can bring Me no shame,*' He also wrote. '*Nay, by My life, it conferreth on Me glory. That which can make Me ashamed is the conduct of such of My followers who profess to love Me, yet in fact follow the Evil One.*'[39]

Such was the measure of Bahá'u'lláh's sufferings in the prison-city of 'Akká.

Notwithstanding the fierce prejudices which assailed them on every side, the Bahá'ís succeeded before long in subduing the hatred of the populace. A war was waged between the forces of character and integrity, and turbulent passions bred by ignorance. In the end victory went to the side which had risen above the plane of conflict, and in submitting its will to a Higher Will, had freed itself of fear and distrust. It gradually dawned upon the officials and the leaders of religion that their Chief Prisoner was not an ordinary man, that they had in their custody a Personage of vastly superior gifts and powers. They became enamoured of His majestic bearing, of His amazing knowledge of human affairs, of His disarming charity and forbearing nature. Their prisoner He was, but a time came when it was almost impossible to realize the fact, or to enforce the harsh and drastic injunctions of the government in Constantinople.

Bahá'ís came from far and wide, and with little difficulty attained the presence of Bahá'u'lláh. High officials of the Ottoman government sought interviews with the Prisoner, to

ay Him their respects. The Muftí of 'Akká, who was once a
igoted opponent, gave Him his allegiance. The new governor,
hmad Big Tawfíq, begged to be allowed to render Him a
ersonal service, and was told by Him to repair, instead, the
queduct outside the town which had become derelict. This
neasure ensured the water supply of 'Akká, and the people
aid that the air of their town had taken a decided turn for the
etter, since Bahá'u'lláh's arrival in their midst. Later, another
overnor, Muṣṭafá Ḍíyá Páshá made it known that should
ahá'u'lláh wish to leave 'Akká for the countryside, He would
ot be prevented.

However nine years elapsed before Bahá'u'lláh left the
onfines of the city walls. 'Abdu'l-Bahá gives us a graphic
ccount of the circumstances of that significant event.
ignificant indeed it was, as it verified a promise uttered by
ahá'u'lláh long before, while still incarcerated in the forbidding
arracks of the prison town. *'Fear not,'* He had written, *'these
oors shall be opened, My tent shall be pitched on Mount Carmel, and
he utmost joy shall be realized.'*

Bahá'u'lláh was very fond of the countryside, but, detained
vithin the cheerless walls of 'Akká, He was barred from the
eauties of nature. A day came when He said, *'I have not gazed
n verdure for nine years. The country is the world of the soul, the city
s the world of bodies.'* Then 'Abdu'l-Bahá knew that the time
ad arrived when it would be possible to end the spell of
mprisonment. Accordingly He went in search of a house in
he plains. Some four miles north of 'Akká, He rented the
esidence of 'Abdu'lláh Páshá. This is the house which we
now as Mazra'ih. He also rented the garden of Na'mayn
vhich lay in the middle of a river, only a short distance from
he city. Later Bahá'u'lláh gave it the name of Riḍván, an
onour reminiscent of that garden outside Baghdád where
Bahá'u'lláh first spoke of His Divine mandate. These abodes
were ready to receive Him, but Bahá'u'lláh, considering Himself

still a prisoner, would not agree to leave the city walls. He maintained that He was not entitled to the freedom of His movements. A second and a third time 'Abdu'l-Bahá repeated His request to His Father, and received the same answer. Next the Muftí of 'Akká, Shaykh 'Alíy-i-Mírí, who was very devoted to Bahá'u'lláh, pleaded with Him: 'God forbid! Who has the power to make you a prisoner. You have kept yourself in prison.' At the end the Shaykh obtained His consent.

After two years at Mazra'ih, Bahá'u'lláh moved His residence to a neighbouring house—the Mansion of Bahjí—built by a man named 'Údí Khammár, and there He lived the remaining years of His life. Whilst Bahá'u'lláh was imprisoned in the citadel, this charming mansion was in the process of construction. Now its owner had fled due to fear of a raging epidemic and the spacious building was vacant. It was rented by 'Abdu'l-Bahá, and afterwards purchased. Bahjí, meaning 'Delight', was near the coast, but far enough from the drab surroundings of 'Akká to be invested with rural beauty. From the windows of His room, Bahá'u'lláh could watch the pure blue of the Mediterranean, the distant minarets of the prison city, and even further, beyond the bay, He could see the dim outline of the gentle slope of Mount Carmel. The Mansion, in all its splendour, stands guard today over the adjoining Shrine which, to the Bahá'ís, is the most sacred spot on the face of the earth, and harbours the mortal remains of Bahá'u'lláh. In its radius one can experience that peace for which one's soul has ever yearned.

Dr. J. E. Esslemont, author of that immortal work, *Bahá'u'lláh and the New Era*, thus describes the life at Bahjí: 'Having in His earlier years of hardship shown how to glorify God in a state of poverty and ignominy, Bahá'u'lláh in His later years at Bahjí showed how to glorify God in a state of honour and affluence. The offerings of hundreds of thousands of devoted followers placed at His disposal large funds which He was called upon to administer. Although His life at Bahjí has been described as truly regal, in the highest sense of the word, yet it must not be imagined that it was characterized by material splendour or extravagance. The Blessed Perfection and His family lived in very simple and modest fashion, and expenditure on selfish luxury was a thing unknown in that household. Near His home the believers prepared a beautiful garden called Riḍván, in which He spent many consecutive days or even weeks, sleeping at night in a little cottage in the garden. Occasionally He went further afield. He made several visits to 'Akká and Haifa, and on more than one occasion pitched His tent on Mount Carmel, as He had predicted when imprisoned in the barracks at 'Akká'.[40]

It was to Bahjí that Edward Granville Browne, the distinguished orientalist and Fellow of Pembroke College, Cambridge, then at the outset of his brilliant academic career, came in April, 1890. Returned home, he committed to paper the impressions he had received: 'So here at *Behjé* was I installed as a guest, in the very midst of all that Bábísm accounts most noble and most holy; and here did I spend five most memorable days, during which I enjoyed unparalleled and unhoped-for opportunities of holding intercourse with those who are the very fountain-heads of that mighty and wondrous spirit which works with invisible but ever-increasing force for the transformation and quickening of a people who slumber in a sleep like unto death. It was in truth a strange and moving experience, but one whereof I despair of conveying any save the feeblest impression. I might, indeed, strive to describe in greater detail the faces and forms which surrounded me, the conversations to which I was privileged to listen, the solemn melodious reading of the sacred books, the general sense of harmony and content which pervaded the place, and the fragrant shady gardens whither in the afternoon we sometimes repaired; but all this was nought in comparison with the spiritual atmosphere with which I was encompassed. ... The spirit which pervades the Bábís is such that it can hardly fail to affect most powerfully all subjected to its influence. It may appall or attract: it cannot be ignored or disregarded. Let those who have not seen disbelieve me if they will; but, should that spirit once reveal itself to them, they will experience an emotion which they are not likely to forget.'[41]

Edward Browne has left us a pen-portrait of Bahá'u'lláh. It is the only one of its kind in existence, and therefore of tremendous value to the student of the Bahá'í Faith. Today a visitor to Bahjí can read this document, before venturing into Bahá'u'lláh's chamber. Thus can one try to recreate in one's mind the interview granted to the English orientalist:

'...my conductor paused for a moment while I removed my shoes. Then with a quick movement of the hand, he withdrew, and, as I passed, replaced the curtain; and I found myself in a large apartment, along the upper end of which ran a low divan, while on the side opposite to the door were placed two or three chairs. Though I dimly suspected whither I was going and whom I was to behold (for no distinct intimation had been given to me), a second or two elapsed ere, with a throb of wonder and awe, I became definitely conscious that the room was not untenanted. In the corner, where the divan met the wall sat a wondrous and venerable figure, crowned with a felt head-dress of the kind called *táj* by dervishes (but of unusual height and make), round the base of which was wound a small white turban. The face of him on whom I gazed I can never forget, though I cannot describe it. Those piercing eyes seemed to read one's very soul; power and authority sat on that ample brow; while the deep lines on the forehead and face implied an age which the jet-black hair and beard flowing down in indistinguishable luxuriance almost to the waist seemed to belie. No need to ask in whose presence I stood, as I bowed myself before one who is the object of a devotion and love which kings might envy and emperors sigh for in vain!

'A mild dignified voice bade me be seated, and then continued:– "*Praise be to God that thou hast attained! ... Thou hast come to see a prisoner and an exile. ... We desire but the good of the world and the happiness of the nations; yet they deem us a stirrer-up of strife and sedition worthy of bondage and banishment. ... That all nations should become one in faith and all men as brothers; that the bonds of affection and unity between the sons of men should be strengthened; that diversity of religion should cease, and differences of race be annulled —what harm is there in this? ... Yet so it shall be; these fruitless strifes, these ruinous wars shall pass away, and the 'Most Great Peace' shall come. ... Do not you in Europe need this also? Is not this that which Christ foretold? ... Yet do we see your kings and rulers lavishing their treasures more freely on means for the destruction of the human race than on that which would conduce to the happiness of mankind. ... These strifes and this bloodshed and discord must cease, and all men be as one kindred and one family. ... Let not a man glory in this, that he loves his country; let him rather glory in this, that he loves his kind ...*"

'Such, so far as I can recall them, were the words which, besides many others, I heard from Behá. Let those who read them consider well with themselves whether such doctrines merit death and bonds, and whether the world is more likely to gain or lose by their diffusion.'[42]

In that year, 1890, Bahá'u'lláh visited Haifa, and pitched His tent on Mount Carmel. To the Mountain of God came the Lord of Hosts, and the prophecies of old as well as His own emphatic promise were fulfilled. He visited Haifa four times and once He raised His tent in the neighbourhood of the Carmelite monastery within which is the Cave of Elijah. There He revealed a Tablet which we know as the *Tablet of Carmel,* majestic and momentous, ringing with joy and with triumph:

'All glory be to this Day, the Day in which the fragrances of mercy have been wafted over all created things, a Day so blest that past ages and centuries can never hope to rival it, a Day in which the Countenance of the Ancient of Days hath turned towards His holy seat. Thereupon the voice of all created things, and beyond them those of the Concourse on high, were heard calling aloud: "Haste Thee, O Carmel, for lo, the light of the Countenance of God, the Ruler of the Kingdom of Names and Fashioner of the heavens, hath been lifted upon thee".

'Seized with transports of joy, and raising high her voice, she thus exclaimed: "May my life be a sacrifice to Thee, inasmuch as Thou hast fixed Thy gaze upon me, hast bestowed upon me Thy bounty, and hast directed towards me Thy steps. Separation from Thee, O Thou Source of everlasting life, hath well nigh consumed me, and my remoteness from Thy presence hath burned away my soul. All praise be to Thee for having enabled me to hearken to Thy call, for having honoured me with Thy footsteps, and for having quickened my soul through the vitalizing fragrance of Thy Day and the thrilling voice of Thy Pen, a voice Thou didst ordain as Thy trumpet-call amidst Thy people ..."

'No sooner had her voice reached that most exalted Spot than We made reply: "Render thanks unto Thy Lord, O Carmel. The fire of thy separation from Me was fast consuming thee, when the ocean of My presence surged before thy face, cheering thine eyes and those of all creation, and filling with delight all things visible and invisible. ... Seize thou the Chalice of Immortality in the name of thy Lord, the All-Glorious, and give thanks unto Him, inasmuch as He, in token of His mercy unto thee, hath turned thy sorrow into gladness, and transmuted thy grief into blissful joy. He, verily, loveth the spot which hath been made the seat of His throne, which His footsteps have trodden, which hath been honoured by His presence, from which He raised His call, and upon which He shed His tears.

' "Call out to Zion, O Carmel, and announce the joyful tidings: He that was hidden from mortal eyes is come.

His all-conquering sovereignty is manifest; His all-encompassing splendour is revealed. ... Ere long will God sail His Ark upon thee, and will manifest the people of Bahá who have been mentioned in the Book of Names ... ".'[43]

One day, Bahá'u'lláh, standing by the side of some lone cypress trees, nearly half-way up the slopes of Mount Carmel, pointed to an expanse of rock immediately below Him and told His Son, 'Abdu'l-Bahá, that on that spot should be built the mausoleum to enshrine the remains of the Báb, the Martyr-Prophet—remains that had been kept in hiding since the second night after July 9th, 1850, the day on which the Báb was shot in the public square of Tabríz. More than a decade had to elapse before 'Abdu'l-Bahá could carry through the mandate laid upon Him by His Father. Today, on the very spot indicated by Bahá'u'lláh, stands a mausoleum of glorious beauty, surmounted by a golden dome reflecting many hues of the sea and sky, and surrounded by gardens that ravish the eyes and enchant the soul. Within that mausoleum the mangled remains of the Martyr-Prophet are laid to rest.

The last years of Bahá'u'lláh's life were devoted to writing and revealing innumerable Tablets, Epistles and Treatises on many and varied subjects of spiritual and educative purport. He was relieved of such cares as His supreme station entailed by the able administration of 'Abdu'l-Bahá, Who shielded Him from the interference of the outside world and met and conversed with the officials of the Government, inquirers and the learned, admitting into the Presence of Bahá'u'lláh only those who had genuine problems to resolve.

It was during the years of confinement within the city walls of 'Akká that He had revealed, besides many other Tablets,

'The Mother Book of His Dispensation', thus styled by the Guardian of the Bahá'í Faith. That was the *Kitáb-i-Aqdas* (The Most Holy Book). Therein He specified the laws and the institutions of His World Order; addressed, admonished and warned the leaders and rulers of men, individually and collectively; exhorted His followers, indeed the generality of mankind, to walk in the paths of righteousness, to be just, to be tolerant, to be truthful, to be loyal, to shun division and conflict, to live in peace.*

The last book which flowed from His creative Pen wa *Epistle to the Son of the Wolf*, a book addressed to a clergyman of Iṣfahán, an inveterate and notorious enemy of the Faith whose greed and schemings resulted in murder and cruel persecution. Here Bahá'u'lláh reiterates His challenge to His detractors. His Call is from God, His trust is in God, and no earthly power can deter Him in His purpose. Herein is also a representative selection from the vast volume of His Writings culled and presented by Himself.

The Writings of Bahá'u'lláh in their range, their scope and their depth, remain unequalled amongst the Scriptures of mankind. We should pause to examine in brief their nature and their purport. That erudite Bahá'í scholar and teacher, Mírza Abu'l-Faḍl† of Gulpáygán‡, classifies them into four categories namely, laws and ordinances; meditations, communes and prayers; interpretations of the sacred scriptures of the past and finally discourses and exordiums. Of the first category he writes: 'Some of them contain laws and regulations whereby the rights and interests of all the nations of the world can be perpetuated, for these statutes are so enacted that they meet the necessities of every land and country, and are acceptable to every man of intelligence. In this universality they resemble

* In the *Kitáb-i-Aqdas* there are laws that concern the individual, and laws tha guard the well-being of society; laws that find immediate application, and law that await the world of the future.

† 1844–1914. ‡ A town in Írán.

the laws of Nature, which secure the progress and development of all peoples; and they will bring about universal union and harmony.'[44] Some of the principal Works of the Author of the Bahá'í Faith have been mentioned in previous pages, and it is impossible to tabulate the rest in this limited account of His life. Bahá'u'lláh states that the volume of His revealed Word totals the Scriptures of the Manifestations preceding Him. We ought to remember the incalculable advantage which the Writings of Bahá'u'lláh possess in relation to the Holy Books of former times. Their originals are extant and well preserved, and future generations will be spared the crushing responsibility of deciding the authenticity of the Works ascribed to the Prophet. Oral tradition finds no place in the Scriptures of the Bahá'í Faith.

Bahá'u'lláh left His human temple on the 29th of May, 1892. A telegram bore the news to the Sulṭán of Turkey: 'The Sun of Bahá has set.' Yet It shines dazzlingly in the full meridian. Its energising and life-bestowing rays continue to revivify the hearts and minds of men, to penetrate the dark clouds of superstition, bigotry and prejudice, to disperse the heavy and oppressive fogs of despair and disillusionment, to shed light upon the baffling problems which bewilder a wayward, fatigued and storm-tossed humanity. Man has essayed to dim Its brilliance, to deny Its potency, to abjure Its gifts, to disparage Its claims—futile and bootless attempts, for the signal proof of the sun remains the sun itself.

Seventy years separate us from the days when Bahá'u'lláh lived amongst men. The Faith which He proclaimed has encircled the globe and marches from triumph to triumph, and the resplendent edifice which He raised stands to offer certitude and peace to a disordered world.

In His Will and Testament, Bahá'u'lláh appointed His eldest Son, Whom we know as 'Abdu'l-Bahá (the Servant of Glory), the Centre of His Covenant with all men, and the sole Expounder of His revealed Word. His name was 'Abbás. His Father referred to Him as the 'Greatest Branch', and spoke of Him as the 'Mystery of God'. Bahá'u'lláh referred to Him also as the 'Master', and so did the Bahá'ís. 'Abdu'l-Bahá was the designation which He chose for Himself, after His Father's ascension.

The Will and Testament of Bahá'u'lláh is indeed a unique document. Never before had a Manifestation of God so explicitly established a Covenant to be the shield and the buttress of His Faith, or so clearly and indubitably named Him Who was to be His authorized successor with power to ward off the machinations of self-seekers, to keep pure and unsullied His Word, to preserve and watch over the unity of His followers, to bar sectarianism and banish corruption. Indeed the Covenant of Bahá'u'lláh is, in the words of 'Abdu'l-Bahá, '*the Sure Handle mentioned from the foundation of the World in the Books, the Tablets and the Scriptures of old.*' '*The pivot of the oneness of mankind,*' 'Abdu'l-Bahá has also said, '*is nothing else but the power of the Covenant.*'

It is on this rock—the rock of the Covenant—that the edifice of the World Order is built. It is this ark, the ark of the Covenant, that has brought the Cause of Bahá'u'lláh safely through storms and hurricanes of unsurpassed intensity. Many a Judas has tried to pierce this shield, the shield of the Covenant, only to find himself in grievous loss.

Bahá'u'lláh wrote in His Will and Testament:

> 'Although the Most High Horizon is devoid of trivial possessions of the earth, We have nevertheless bequeathed unto Our heirs a noble and peerless heritage within the treasure-house of trust and resignation. We have left no treasure nor have We added to man's pains. ... In bearing

hardships and tribulations and in revealing verses and expounding proofs, it has been the purpose of this oppressed One to extinguish the fire of hate and animosity, that haply the horizons of the hearts of mankind may be illumined with the light of concord and attain real tranquillity. ... Truly I say, the tongue is for mentioning that which is good; do not defile it by evil speech. ... Man's station is great. ... This is a Day great and blessed. Whatsoever was hidden in man is today being revealed. The station of man is great, were he to cling to truth and righteousness and be firm and steadfast in the Cause. ... O people of the world! The religion of God is to create love and unity; do not make it the cause of enmity and discord. All that is regarded by men of insight and the people of most lofty outlook as the means for safeguarding and effecting the peace and tranquillity of man, has flowed from the Supreme Pen. ... Do not make the cause of order a cause for disorder, nor the means for disunity. It is hoped that the people of Bahá will observe the sacred verse: "Say, all are created by God". This lofty utterance is like unto water for quenching the fire of hate and hostility which is hidden and stored in men's hearts and minds. This single utterance will cause the various sects and creeds to attain the light of true unity. Verily, He speaketh truth and guideth to the right path; and He is the Mighty, the Glorious, the Omnipotent. ...'

Bahá'u'lláh had left the mortal phase. Many they were who came to mourn Him. They did not bear allegiance to Him, they could not see in Him the Redeemer of Mankind, yet they knew that a great Being had gone from their midst. They were from diverse backgrounds and sects and Faiths—officials and leading figures and priests, learned men and poets, rich and poor, Druzes, Sunní and Shí'ih Muslims, Christians and Jews. From other cities such as Damascus and Aleppo and Cairo, they sent their eulogies and poems and tributes. And Bahá'u'lláh, at the time of His ascension, was still a prisoner of the Turkish government. No imperial edict of the Sultán had set Him free.

How different was this day of His ascension, when the plain stretching between the city of 'Akká and the Mansion of Bahjí teemed with crowds who came to pay Him homage and lament their loss, from that far-off day nearly twenty-four summers before when crowds had awaited His arrival at the seashore of 'Akká, to deride and insult Him. Total, unmitigated defeat seemed to be His fate then, and now all triumph was His.

Indeed, how strange and awe-inspiring had been the contrasts of His sojourn among men, particularly in the Holy Land.

Brutally insulted in His native province, shorn of all earthly possessions, which He had in abundance, twice consigned to a prison of thieves and desperadoes, four times set on the road to exile, basely betrayed by His own brother whom He had endeavoured to protect, forced to seek the solitude of bare mountains, venomously and ferociously assailed and denounced and opposed by hordes of the mighty and the powerful and the insignificant alike, He had stood His ground with a certitude and a constancy which no adversity could shake and no cataclysm could thwart. And upon a swelling number of faithful adherents He conferred that supreme gift which Jesus had spoken of to Nicodemus when the Jewish nobleman sought Him in the dead of night—the gift of second birth. He touched the hearts of men, and He won their allegiance by His Divine power. His followers were not alone in feeling its sweep and its command. Many who had denied Him and reviled Him and openly contended with Him, were eventually subdued by the charm, the majesty, the kindliness, the radiance of His Being. Indeed there were many amongst these erstwhile adversaries who, without enrolling in the ranks of His followers, bore testimony to His supremacy, and lent their support in His defence.

And where was 'Abdu'l-'Azíz of Turkey, the Sulṭán who decreed His exile and incarceration? Where was Napoleon, the Emperor of the French who disdained His summons and waxed proud before Him? Beaten, deposed, sunk in ignominy. Náṣiri'd-Dín of Persia, who had cast Him out of His native land, and who had made Him take the road to exile twice, fell only five years after the ascension of Bahá'u'lláh, before the bullets of an avenger, on the very eve of his golden jubilee. The records of history amply show that great was the fall of anyone, mighty or low alike, who dared to challenge Bahá'u'lláh, and gainsay His sovereignty. No one has opposed Bahá'u'lláh and raised his hand to injure His Cause and His followers, and has escaped shame, doom and degradation.

This is an attempt to catch the ocean in a diminutive cup, to gaze at the orb through plain glass. Far, very far from man's effort must be an adequate portrayal of a Manifestation of the Qualities and Attributes of Almighty God. And here we deal with the life of One Whose advent implies the 'coming of age of the entire human race', and under Whose dominion the earth will become one fatherland.

THE WORD MADE FLESH

God is unknowable. He is infinite; we are finite, and the finite cannot encompass the infinite. But God created man in His own image, in the image of His qualities and attributes. He created man because He loved his creation.

> 'O Son of Man!' writes Bahá'u'lláh, 'Veiled in My immemorial being and in the ancient eternity of My essence, I knew My love for thee; therefore I created thee, have engraved on thee Mine image and revealed to thee My beauty.'[45]

The Manifestation of God

So that man should know Him and love Him, and do His will, God has from age to age manifested Himself to men, in a human temple.

Again Bahá'u'lláh writes,

> 'The door of the knowledge of the Ancient of Days being thus closed in the face of all beings, the Source of infinite grace . . . hath caused those luminous Gems of Holiness to appear out of the realm of the spirit, in the noble form of the human temple, and be made manifest unto all men, that They may impart unto the world the mysteries of the unchangeable Being, and tell of the subtleties of His imperishable Essence. These sanctified Mirrors, these Daysprings of ancient glory are one and all the Exponents on earth of Him Who is the central Orb of the universe, its Essence and ultimate Purpose. From Him proceed their knowledge and power; from Him is derived Their sovereignty. The beauty of Their countenance is but a reflection of His image, and Their revelation a sign of His deathless glory. They are the Treasuries of divine knowledge, and the Repositories of celestial wisdom. Through Them is transmitted a grace that is infinite, and by Them is revealed the light that can never fade.'[46]

The Manifestations of God are the '*Word* (*of God*) *made flesh.*' They reveal God to man. Through Them and by Them man comes to know God, and learns the purpose of God. It is only through His Manifestations that God can be known. In Them nothing can be seen but the glory and the power, the majesty and the will of the Godhead. Jesus said that whoever had seen Him had seen the Father, he who had known Him had known God. Every road to the Creator of the universe is barred, save that through His Manifestations, through those divine Figures, those exalted Beings Whom we know as the Founders of the religions of mankind. Therefore Jesus said: '*I am the way, and the truth, and the life: no man cometh unto the Father, but by me.*'[47]

The Manifestation of God links the world of God with the world of man. He is a human being, completely and totally possessed of humanity, sharing in full the life of man, having the same sorrows, the same pains, the same joys. But His reality is the reality of the Holy Spirit. He is the chosen vehicle of God's revelation. His being is like a perfect, stainless mirror reflecting to mankind the reality of the Godhead. Hold a mirror, 'Abdu'l-Bahá tells us, to the sun, and in it you will find reflected the shining brilliant orb of the firmament with augmented heat and augmented light. By this simile, He illustrates the reflection of the reality of the Godhead in a human temple. God and man meet in the being of the Manifestation of God, who thus becomes the link between the world of the Creator and the world of the created.

The Second Birth

The first divine hypothesis, 'Abdu'l-Bahá has said, is the appearance of the Manifestations of God. History attests this fact, and history should be read in terms of Their appearance, Their teaching, Their influence, Their achievement. They are the makers of history. Without reference to Them, history shows no conscious purpose, no direction, no intrinsic meaning, no ultimate goal. The Manifestation of God not only directs man to the path of God, not only tells him what God has meant for him, and what God intends him to do, but He energises and revitalises his life, uplifts his spirit, confers upon him a 'new birth'.

In the dead of night, the fourth gospel tells us, Nicodemus, a prominent man and leader of his people, went to see Jesus. What questions he put to Jesus St. John does not tell us. But it is not hard to guess. Nicodemus was a ruler amongst the Jews, and the problem of his people was the problem of Rome. Here were the people chosen and exalted by God, custodians of monotheism in a world of idol-worshippers, subjected and scorned by followers of pagan beliefs, practisers of pagan rites. How could they throw off this hated, unbearable yoke? This was the problem of Nicodemus and his people, but all that Jesus would tell him was that he should be born again. And this Nicodemus could not understand.

But Peter understood it—Peter, the simple fisherman, so simple, 'Abdu'l-Bahá tells us, that he could not keep count of the days of the week. He was not a man of substance. He was a stranger to fame and position. One day Jesus told this simple, obscure fisherman to leave his nets and follow Him. Unhesitatingly Peter did this, and yet he knew nothing of what Jesus had come to teach. The Sermon on the Mount had yet to be preached. The mysteries and the glories of the Kingdom had yet to be spoken of. Miracles had yet to be witnessed. But the soul of Peter responded to the call of Jesus. He followed Jesus, and his Master made of him a new creation. On him He conferred a 'new birth'. By submitting to the power and the command of the Manifestation of God, Peter partook of His glory, was given insight and knowledge and understanding. In that world from which Peter had come, there were scores and hundreds of men outstanding in various fields of human achievement. In their eyes and in their estimation, Peter and his like had no significance. But they and their accomplishments have long been forgotten, whilst Peter lives in countless hearts. His name is blessed and has gone round the whole globe. This is how a Manifestation of God performs the greatest of all His miracles.

> 'O Lord! Should the breaths of the Holy Spirit confirm the weakest of creatures,' says 'Abdu'l-Bahá in a prayer, 'he shall attain to the highest station of greatness and shall possess anything he desireth. Indeed Thou hast assisted Thy servants in the past, and they were the weakest of Thy creatures . . . and the most insignificant of those who lived upon the earth; but through Thy sanction and potency they took precedence over the most glorious of Thy people and the most noble of mankind. Whereas formerly they were as moths, they became as royal falcons.'[48]

Elsewhere He speaks of gnats turned into eagles.

The Manifestation of God is God's Vicar on earth, and it is by the grace and the guidance which He brings to mankind that gnats can be turned into eagles. Wielding the authority and possessing the power that They do, the Manifestations of God achieve prodigies that are spoken of as miracles. Nothing can be impossible to Them. Indeed They can heal the sick and raise the dead. But these miracles cannot be convincing proofs of Their claim that They have come to man with a message and a mandate from God. How many were those who saw such miracles with their own eyes? But having seen the outward appearance they failed to see the inner purport. Some shrugged their shoulders and went their way; some accused the Manifestation of God of sorcery; some denied the reality of what they had witnessed; some tried to explain it away, and in future ages they relegated it to the realm of myths.

Furthermore the followers of one Manifestation, whilst attributing such miracles to the Founder of their own Faith, maintain that miracles said to have been performed by a Manifestation appearing in a later age, are pure fabrication. A Muslim accepts as true report the story of a miracle ascribed to Jesus. But a Christian is not prepared to admit the validity of any account that puts Muḥammad on the same plane with Jesus. A Zoroastrian rejects miracles both of Jesus and of Muḥammad. Such deeds can be easily denied. But the person of Peter, the fisherman of Galilee, cannot be denied. Raising him to the heights which he attained is the hallmark of the power and the achievement of a Manifestation of God.

A youth of seventeen became the bearer of the Tablet which Bahá'u'lláh addressed to the Sháh of Persia. 'Badí' '—the wonderful—was the designation which Bahá'u'lláh later conferred upon him. This heroic soul, although so young in years, had led a life which was not commendable, and had brought great disappointment to his family. Then he turned towards 'Akká, where Bahá'u'lláh was confined in its grim barracks, and he started walking. All his hopes were centred on 'Akká. He reached it, he entered the presence of Bahá'u'lláh, he was entrusted with the Tablet addressed to the Sháh. And he started walking back. Outside the capital city of Persia he awaited the despotic ruler of his country, and when he came face to face with Násiri'd-Dín Sháh, this boy, calm and composed, barely seventeen years of age, hailed the monarch with these words: 'O King! I have come to thee from Sheba with a weighty message.' He was arrested, branded and tortured. He never flinched. A photograph exists of him with his torturers. It vividly portrays the dignity and the faith of a martyr. And this was the same youth whose life had lacked so much that was desirable. In him, said Bahá'u'lláh, '*the spirit of might and power was breathed.*'*

* See page 41.

Muḥammad had an uncle named Ḥamzih, a fierce warrior, proud and arrogant. He had not accepted the mission of the Prophet, but Muḥammad was his nephew, and the Arab's sense of clan loyalty was intense. For years Muḥammad was subjected to pitiless, unceasing persecution, and Ḥamzih would, whenever feasible, come forward to defend and protect his nephew. Once, while away on a hunting trip, the people of Mecca inflicted severe injuries on the person of the Prophet. The hunter returned home dishevelled and fatigued, to find his wife in great distress. She was a follower of her husband's nephew, and now she took her husband to task. How could he remain silent when his nephew was so grossly insulted and so brutally maltreated! Ḥamzih sallied forth immediately in search of Muḥammad and brusquely demanded to be told the names of the persecutors. Ḥamzih was impatient and Muḥammad was unyielding. Then the Prophet suggested to His uncle that prior to learning the names of the persecutors and setting out to wreak vengeance upon them, he should repeat the words which every Muslim utters in declaration of his faith—'I testify that there is no God but God. I testify that Muḥammad is the Messenger of God.' Ḥamzih did so in haste, and then Muḥammad told him that no one who had uttered those weighty words could nurture any thought of revenge. The arrogant, ferocious man was subdued, and in an instant he recognised the truth of his Nephew's claims. Thereafter Ḥamzih bore slights and insults with faith and fortitude.

Such is the mysterious power of the Manifestation of God. Thus does He change the hearts of men. Thus does He call forth a new creation.

God's Chosen One

The Manifestation of God does not willingly, knowingly and consciously seek the station which is His; He does not undergo a rigorous spiritual discipline with that intent. The Revelation which comes to Him from God is unsought. The choice belongs to God. When the Manifestation of God becomes conscious of His true identity, of His Mission, of the mandate given to Him by His Creator, He is puzzled. Why did God choose Him to be His Vicar on this earth, the vehicle of His Revelation? The Báb, Martyr-Prophet and the Herald of the Faith of Bahá'u'lláh, states that the appearance of a Manifestation of God is preordained. The emergence of the Infinite into the finite, for such is the nature of Revelation, the advent of the Unchangeable and the Everlasting into the ephemeral, the appearance of the dazzling splendour of God in a human temple, is not a matter of chance, a haphazard occurrence. Neither is it whimsical. There is a pattern ever unfolding from age to age. There is a definite intent, a definite purpose at work. The World of God is timeless, but its linking with the world of man through the World of Revelation is subject to the dictates of time. The Báb, referring to His own declaration, His own assumption of prophethood, which took place at two hours and eleven minutes after the sunset of May 22nd, 1844, asserts that this hour was determined from the beginning that hath no beginning. Since Revelation is progressive, and the Manifestations of God—His Messengers to mankind—come from age to age, Their advent is determined in relation to time.

It is in the Revelation of Bahá'u'llah that for the first time in the religious experience of mankind, the reality, the station, the function and the mission of the Manifestation of God, are made unequivocally clear. All the arguments and counter-arguments of human invention pale into insignificance in the light of Bahá'u'lláh's exposition. In this light one can see the majestic rhythm of the march of history. Purpose—conscious, rational purpose becomes evident. The logic of circumstances is laid bare. History is seen as a stupendous drama, unfolded from one act to another—each act and each chapter defined and determined by the magnetic and vivifying powers of a Manifestation of God, Who brings that measure of guidance required for the age in which He appears. The Manifestation of God guides, leads and directs, but His message and His teachings are qualified by the degree of growth reached by Man at that particular epoch. The wholeness and oneness of religion is established as incontrovertible fact. One refuses to accept the existence of fundamental conflict amongst the religions of mankind. The law of evolution is found to be applicable to religion, which ceases to be divorced from life, and in fact causes the evolution of society. The interdependence of the diverse Faiths of mankind is well understood. No longer will man concede a cleavage between the spiritual and the temporal.

Therefore it follows that the rise of every civilization is due to the spiritual dynamic released by a Manifestation of God and the fall of every civilization is caused by the stagnation of the same dynamic in the course of time. 'Abdu'l-Bahá traces, in the world of the spirit, the same seasons that exist in the world of nature. There is a spiritual springtide—the days of re-awakenning and of seed-sowing—followed by the period corresponding to summer in the physical world, when growth is well evident and the seeds sown erstwhile, having taken root and sprouted in human hearts and minds, flourish in full verdure; next arrives the time of autumn, when the harvest is reaped and the civilization thus reared yields its fairest fruits; at last winter sets in, everything is by then formalised, the spirit of search and adventure is dead, minds and hearts are frigid and cold, chained and bound; gone is ease and freedom of movement, all is cumbersome, all is deadening. Once the cycle is complete, springtide returns in its full glory.

Religious truth is not absolute, but relative—relative to the age and the time in which it is revealed. Every principle and every law which a Manifestation of God gives to mankind, is the translation into terms relevant to the age and applicable to the conditions of that age, of truths and qualities which in their absolute reside with the Godhead. As man progresses, as man's horizons, be they physical, intellectual or spiritual are widened, more and more of the truths and qualities which in their infinite and absolute essence exist in God, are revealed to man.

'Abdu'l-Bahá places the teachings and the precepts of the Manifestations of God in two categories: those that are eternal and ever-abiding, not subject to change and annulment, and those that are temporary and ephemeral, entirely related to the exigencies and requirements of a particular age and era. The first category comprises eternal verities such as love, justice, charity and mercy. The second category embraces such laws as those that govern marriage and divorce, penalties and punishment, inheritance and commerce. Although these laws and prescriptions are subject to change, they form an integral part of any Revelation, inasmuch as they represent the application of eternal truths to the life of man both individually and collectively.

Again 'Abdu'l-Bahá, speaking of the laws and precepts revealed by a Manifestation of God, says, '*The laws of God are not impositions of will, or of power or pleasure, but the resolutions of truth, reason and justice.*'

No Manifestation of God has ever come to man to say that the Message which He is imparting to the world is of His own invention. No Manifestation of God has set out to seek a panacea. In the early life of no Manifestation of God, wherever the evidence is available, can we find any preoccupation with a prophetic mission. Indeed the story of His first intimation of His divine call, indicates considerable surprise and soul-searching. Moses encountered a burning bush from which the Voice of God reached Him. And He was puzzled. He was told to go to Egypt, a country He had fled. He hesitated. He argued.

'And Moses said unto the Lord, *O my Lord, I am not eloquent, neither heretofore, nor since Thou hast spoken unto Thy servant; but I am slow of speech, and of a slow tongue.*'[49]

When Jesus was baptized by His cousin, John, He saw the skies open, a dove descend, and He heard the voice of God calling Him His Son, His best beloved. And He left John and the crowds and went straight away into the wilderness. There a mighty battle raged in His soul.

'And Jesus, being full of the Holy Ghost, returned from Jordan, and was led by the Spirit into the wilderness, being forty days tempted of the devil. And in those days He did eat nothing: and when they were ended, he afterward hungered.'[50]

There in the wilderness the Being of Jesus became one with the Christ. The human ego was subdued; that was the purport of being tempted by the devil. Had Jesus been preparing Himself for Messiahship, why should He, after undergoing baptism and hearing the call of God, have betaken Himself to the wilderness, there to engage in an awesome struggle, in which His victory was to yield himself completely and totally to the Will of God? Indeed the evidence is clear that Jesus, until the time of His baptism, had not contemplated nor designed His own Messiahship.

Muḥammad was noted for His piety and His integrity. He was given the title of Al-Amín—the trusted One. It was His wont to spend a month in the course of the year at Mount Hira, close to Mecca, in prayer and meditation. But He was neither a hermit nor a recluse. On the contrary He was well involved in the affairs of this world. By all accounts He was a successful merchant. One day in the solitude of the hillside the angel Gabriel appeared to Him. A tablet was held out to Him and He was bidden to read. Muḥammad was illiterate. He could not read nor write, and He was bewildered. Then He was told to read in the Name of His Lord, and He found Himself able to read. Even more bewildered He ran home to His wife and told her what He had experienced and asked to be covered by His mantle. But now He knew that God had chosen Him to be His Messenger. His wife, Khadíjih, was the first to believe in Him.

Muḥammad, the illiterate, was speaking words of unsurpassed beauty and eloquence, words vibrant with life and power. He never claimed that those words and verses were His. They came to Him from God, He told His people. Muḥammad had not sought prophethood. His mandate came to Him from God.

To the Sháh of Persia, Bahá'u'lláh wrote:

> 'O King! I was but a man like others, asleep upon My couch, when lo, the breezes of the All-Glorious were wafted over Me, and taught Me the knowledge of all that hath been. This thing is not from Me, but from One Who is Almighty and All-Knowing. And He bade Me lift up My voice between earth and heaven, and for this there befell Me what hath caused the tears of every man of understanding to flow. The learning current amongst men I studied not; their schools I entered not. Ask of the city wherein I dwelt, that thou mayest be well assured that I am not of them who speak falsely. This is but a leaf which the winds of the will of thy Lord, the Almighty, the All-Praised, have stirred. Can it be still when the tempestuous winds are blowing? Nay, by Him Who is the Lord of all Names and Attributes! They move it as they list.'[51]

Addressing the concourse of men, Bahá'u'lláh says,

> 'God is My witness, O people! I was asleep on My couch, when lo, the Breeze of God wafting over Me roused Me from My slumber. His quickening Spirit revived Me, and My tongue was unloosed to voice His Call. Accuse Me not of having transgressed against God. Behold Me, not with your eyes but with Mine. Thus admonisheth you He Who is the Gracious, the All-Knowing. Think ye, O people, that I hold within My grasp the control of God's ultimate Will and Purpose? Far be it from Me to advance such claim. To this I testify before God, the Almighty, the Exalted, the All-Knowing, the All-Wise. Had the ultimate destiny of God's Faith been in Mine hands, I would never have consented, even though for one moment, to manifest Myself unto you, nor would I have allowed one word to fall from My lips. Of this God Himself is, verily, a witness.'[52]

It was when He was chained and fettered in the darksome, pestilential dungeon of Ṭihrán that Bahá'u'lláh became conscious of His Mission.

> 'While engulfed in tribulations,' He wrote, 'I heard a most wondrous, a most sweet voice, calling above My head. Turning My face, I beheld a Maiden—the embodiment of the remembrance of the name of My Lord—suspended in the air before Me. So rejoiced was she in her very soul that her countenance shone with the ornament of the good-pleasure of God, and her cheeks glowed with the brightness of the All-Merciful. Betwixt earth and heaven she was raising a call which captivated the hearts and minds of men. She was imparting to both My inward and outer being tidings which rejoiced My soul, and the souls of God's honoured servants. Pointing with her finger unto My head, she addressed all who are in heaven and all who are on earth, saying: "By God! This is the Best-Beloved of the worlds, and yet ye comprehend not. This is the Beauty of God amongst you, and the power of His sovereignty within you, could ye but understand. This is the Mystery of God and His Treasure, the Cause of God and His glory unto all who are in the kingdoms of Revelation and of creation, if ye be of them that perceive." '[53]

And this is His further testimony to that experience, which is far above our ken and understanding:

> 'During the days I lay in the prison of Ṭihrán, though the galling weight of the chains and the stench-filled air allowed Me but little sleep, still in those infrequent moments of slumber I felt as if something flowed from the crown of My head over My breast, even as a mighty torrent that precipitateth itself upon the earth from the summit of a lofty mountain. Every limb of My body would, as a result, be set afire. At such moments My tongue recited what no man could bear to hear.'[54]

What is the nature of this experience which Bahá'u'lláh has so succinctly and so vividly related? How does Revelation come from God to His Messenger? By what token does the Manifestation of God recognise the validity of His experience? These are questions to which we can never give answers. We would have to be of the same stature and of the same exalted rank as the Manifestation to comprehend these mighty events. That stature and that rank remain exclusively the domain of Those Whom God chooses to make the Vehicles of His Revelation, the Dawning-Places of His Qualities and Attributes, His Manifestations unto men. Just as no Prophet has purposely and knowingly sought that station, likewise no man, however advanced in perception, however high in spiritual attainments, however pious and virtuous, can ever hope to attain to it by his own exertions. The greatest mystics amongst men have never been able to attain the station of Christ. It is rank effrontery and the peak of self-delusion for man even to imagine that he can will himself to be a Manifestation of God. There are three well-defined, well-demarcated worlds or spheres, separate and distinct, yet linked and indissolubly bound: the world of God (the world of the Creator); the world of *logos* (the world of Manifestation); and the world of man (the world of the created). The world of Manifestation links the world of God with the world of man; and it is God, not man, Who determines Who that link shall be.

The Evolution of Religion

From time immemorial, God has sent His Messengers to mankind, and as long as man lives on this planet and has physical existence here, God will manifest Himself in a human temple. By asserting this fact, the Bahá'í Faith disclaims finality for itself. Indeed, Bahá'u'lláh states in no uncertain terms that other dispensations will succeed His. That no revealed religion can be a false religion is another emphatic statement of the

Bahá'i Faith. It is maintained that although there have been false prophets, and although for a period of time a false claim to prophethood may endure, a false teaching will not last. In the course of time a religion may suffer corruption, its pristine purity may be lost, its light may be dimmed, but its original truth will forever remain. No religion practised and followed by any grouping of mankind, no matter how overtaken it may be by alien creeds and alien rites, no matter how superimposed it may be by man-made interpretations and man-made doctrines, can be labelled a false religion. The most primitive forms of religion still extant in the world must have had their divine Founders, Who came in remote antiquity. No records are left of Them, and Their names are forgotten. But vague memories persist.

We have to differentiate between religions and ecclesiastical organizations with their divisions and sub-divisions. No religion is false, although ensuing fissions may be misguided. Revelation comes from God, religion is founded by a Manifestation of God; but tearing the heart out of religion, polluting the life-giving waters of faith, promoting division and strife and conflict, are all the work of man.

The clear, logical exposition of the process of religious evolution given to the world by Bahá'u'lláh, calls for a reorientation of human thinking. Mankind is now coming of age, and the mature man needs to know, and can comprehend, this scintillating truth now revealed by Bahá'u'lláh. The Manifestation of God, Who partakes of divine knowledge, comes to the world from age to age. He sets the pace of growth and progress. For Him neither time nor space exist. To Him the whole process of human evolution is an open book, continuous and unchaptered. But we human beings are the materials of the evolutionary process. We move and grow within defined chapters. The content and the tempo of each chapter is determined by the Manifestation of God. He is the spiritual Architect, and designs the 'shape of things to come'. The Manifestation of God is not just an idealist, an utopian dreamer, a wishful thinker, a visionary, merely an illumined seer. Neither is He a political scientist, an economist, a sociologist. The Manifestation of God is, in the words of St. John, 'the Word made flesh'. He is the *logos* incarnate, the 'skilled Physician' of human relationships.

Immortality of Man

The reality of man is a spiritual reality, and the Manifestation of God is the creator of the spiritual atmosphere from which man, the real man, draws his substance. '*Man shall not live by bread alone, but by every word that proceedeth out of the mouth of God.*' It is this spiritual food, the '*bread of life*', the divine teachings, which the Manifestation of God provides for man whenever He appears.

All the Faiths of mankind have pronounced man to be indestructible, immortal. His life is not confined to the short span allotted to him on this earth. There are worlds upon worlds beyond the grave. This is how Bahá'u'lláh describes the state and the condition of the soul of man:

> 'Know thou that the soul of man is exalted above, and is independent of all infirmities of body or mind. That a sick person showeth signs of weakness is due to the hindrances that interpose themselves between his soul and his body, for the soul itself remaineth unaffected by any bodily ailments. Consider the light of the lamp. Though an external object may interfere with its radiance, the light itself continueth to shine with undiminished power. In like manner, every malady afflicting the body of man is an impediment that preventeth the soul from manifesting its inherent might and power. When it leaveth the body, however, it will evince such ascendancy, and reveal such influence as no force on earth can equal. Every pure, every

refined and sanctified soul will be endowed with tremendous power, and shall rejoice with exceeding gladness.'[55]

And again:

'And now concerning thy question regarding the soul of man and its survival after death. Know thou of a truth that the soul, after its separation from the body, will continue to progress until it attaineth the presence of God, in a state and condition which neither the revolution of ages and centuries, nor the changes and chances of this world, can alter. It will endure as long as the Kingdom of God, His sovereignty, His dominion and power will endure. It will manifest the signs of God and His attributes, and will reveal His loving kindness and bounty ... The nature of the soul after death can never be described, nor is it meet and permissible to reveal its whole character to the eyes of men. The Prophets and Messengers of God have been sent down for the sole purpose of guiding mankind to the straight Path of Truth. The purpose underlying their revelation hath been to educate all men, that they may, at the hour of death, ascend, in the utmost purity and sanctity and with absolute detachment, to the throne of the Most High. The light which these souls radiate is responsible for the progress of the world and the advancement of its peoples. They are like unto leaven which leaveneth the world of being, and constitute the animating force through which the arts and wonders of the world are made manifest ... All things must needs have a cause, a motive power, an animating principle. These souls and symbols of detachment have provided, and will continue to provide, the supreme moving impulse in the world of being. ... When the soul attaineth the Presence of God, it will assume the form that best befitteth its immortality and is worthy of its celestial habitation.'[56]

'Know, verily, that the soul is a sign of God, a heavenly gem whose reality the most learned of men hath failed to grasp, and whose mystery no mind, however acute, can ever hope to unravel. It is the first among all created things to declare the excellence of its Creator, the first to recognize His glory, to cleave to His truth, and to bow down in adoration before Him.'[57]

Rejected by Man

No Manifestation of God has ever found ready and immediate acceptance amongst the peoples of the world. He is invariably denied and opposed and rejected. He usually comes from lowly and humble origins. True it is that Gautama, the Buddha, was the son of a king, and in our age the Manifestation of God was the son of a king's minister. But Moses was a member of an enslaved and oppressed race, also a fugitive from justice. Yet the Ten Commandments, which this fugitive from justice gave to His people, stand today at the basis of the codes of law of every civilized nation on earth. Jesus was a member of a subject and oppressed race. He was an obscure Galilean, presumably a carpenter by trade, and had no connection with either the Sadducees or the Pharisees, the leaders of His people. Muḥammad is usually referred to as a camel-driver. His family was prominent and highly esteemed, but he was orphaned, and the uncle whose charge He was, was exceedingly poor. The Qur'án clearly states that Muḥammad was illiterate. The Báb was the son of a mercer of Shíráz, orphaned like His Forebear, the Arabian Prophet, and brought up by a maternal uncle. Bahá'u'lláh was the son of a minister of the court of Persia, and enjoyed great riches. But ranging Himself on the side of the Prophet of Shíráz, He forfeited both His wealth and His social status.

Those who first respond to the call of a Manifestation of God are also of humble origin. It is generally so, although there are notable exceptions. It is by the sacrifice of souls whom the world usually holds to be of no account that a Faith nourishes its roots and flourishes. How did their contemporaries regard the disciples of Christ? Amongst them were fishermen, even a tax-collector. The first to believe in the Mission of Muḥammad were Khadíjih, His wife; His cousin, 'Alí, a boy hardly thirteen years of age; and Zayd, a slave. And those who sought the Báb were mostly students of theology, though in their ranks were giants, and later a few of the most outstanding amongst the divines of the land became followers of the Báb. Even more, they joyously gave their lives in His path and suffered glorious martyrdom.

The very fact that ordinary people come to believe with their whole beings in the Manifestation of God, rouses the ire of those who consider themselves the custodians of religious truth. Indeed, they are the first to denounce the Manifestation of God. They do so because they are afraid. What did the people of Jerusalem do on the day Jesus entered their city, the day which is called Palm Sunday? They went out with palm leaves to welcome Him. They gave Him a royal welcome. They had seen the miracles of healing performed, or they had heard of them. They had no conception of the station of Jesus. Indeed, Jesus had not told them who He was. More than that, He had forbidden His disciples to make public what they knew to be the truth. From the day that Peter had recognized Him and told Him that He was the Christ, the Son of the living God, that injunction had been laid upon them. The people of Jerusalem who went out with such zeal and such joy to escort Jesus into their city were welcoming, in their own estimation, a good Rabbi, a holy man, a worker of miracles, a healer and a comforter. But those who wielded spiritual power, those who were the custodians of the law, those to whom the maintenance of their position meant not only the preservation of their high rank, but the ensurance of law and order, saw the implications of the career which Jesus had pursued, realized that only the Messiah could knowingly embark on that course, and took fright. Had they not seen that Jesus was indeed not only the light of Israel, but the light of the world, they would not have concerned themselves with plotting and planning His extinction.

Jesus had already spoken of them and their like. He who in ignorance sins against the Son of Man is forgiven, but He who sins against the Holy Ghost is eternally condemned. 'Eternally,' the Báb tells us, signifies the duration of the Dispensation. He who sins against the Holy Ghost is the man who knows that the Manifestation of God is indeed from God and sent by God, yet rejects Him. He sees the light and calls upon darkness to be his guide. He purposely sets out to extinguish the light. Such a man was Cain. Such were those men who took counsel to destroy Jesus. Such men were those who for thirteen years constituted the spearhead of opposition to Muḥammad, and finally gathered to devise His death. Such a man was Judas Iscariot. Such a man was Azal, Bahá'u'lláh's half-brother, and the Judas of His days. Those who flocked to the courtyard of Pontius Pilate in the early morning of Good Friday and asked for the release of a convicted criminal whilst demanding the death of Jesus, were not in the category of those who sin against the Holy Ghost. But their religious mentors were.

Leaders of religion oppose and persecute the Manifestation of God. So do the leaders of the state. They also take fright. They fear sedition: whereas no Manifestation of God has ever contemplated or designed violent upheaval of the social and the political order. Moses defied the might of Egypt not to overthrow the kingdom of the Pharaohs, but to take His own people, as bidden by God, out of captivity. Christ did not scheme rebellion against Rome. He knew that that way did not lie the salvation of His people. The Jews, in their intense yearning to break the hated yoke of Rome, had thought of their Messiah as a scion of the House of David, arising with kingly might, smiting down with the power of God, sitting in full splendour upon the Throne of David. But the prophecies which had led them to this expectation had a symbolic import.

Had Jesus made Himself the leader of revolt against Rome, instead of but twelve disciples, He would have had an army of zealous adherents behind Him. But He persistently refused to take that course. His opponents went out of their way to trick Him into making a pronouncement which could be construed as incitement to rebellion. He emphatically refused to comply, and gave them an answer which has to this day kept the Christian world arguing and differing over its implications. '*Render therefore unto Caesar the things which are Caesar's; and unto God the things that are God's*,'[58] He said.

Christ did not envisage uprising and revolt against Rome as the means to His end, which was the salvation of His people. His words to Nicodemus, quoted before, indicate that His way was a different one. Yet His opponents brought about His crucifixion by playing upon the fears of the Roman governor. Pontius Pilate was thoroughly alarmed. A squabble amongst the Jews over messianic claims and attitudes to law and doctrine, He would tolerate. But any hint of possible civil disorder and defiance of the Roman overlordship, He would not let go unheeded. His own position was at stake. How would Caesar treat him were he to set free a man accused of harbouring and fostering designs against Rome? So he decreed the death of Jesus.

The Arabia to which Muḥammad spoke was not a political unit. But Mecca, His home-town, had a special place. People came there from near and far to worship the idols that Mecca housed. Those who ruled over Mecca were greatly concerned for the prestige of their city. Muḥammad, they told themselves, was bent on destroying the idols that gave them status, and brought them both wealth and honour. Muḥammad, they said, must be prevented at all costs. They intended to put Him to death. Their resolve was strengthened by the knowledge that He had entered into a covenant with a deputation from Yathrib, later named Medina—the city of the Prophet. It was then that Muḥammad had to flee His home-town.

The Báb had no design on the state and its security. He did not envisage establishing His own temporal rule, although such was the expectation of the people. He came as the Twelfth Imám, the Mihdí (Mahdí), whose advent the Shí'ihs yearned and prayed for. When Manúchihr Khán, the governor of Iṣfahán, a rich, influential official of the state, offered to put his entire fortune and his not inconsiderable army at the disposal of the Báb, to march on Ṭihrán and persuade the Sháh to embrace the new Faith, He Who was the Mihdí, the Qá'im, to Whom in the estimation of the Shí'ihs dominion and sovereignty rightly belonged, kindly but firmly refused the offer. Yet Ḥájí Mírzá Áqásí, the corrupt grand vizier, took fright and prevailed upon his weak and vacillating royal master to decline a meeting with the Báb. It was the State that kept the Báb a prisoner, and finally had Him shot.

Bahá'u'lláh suffered four banishments and two terms of incarceration at the hands of two tyrannical kings. He it was Who stilled the passions of the followers of the Báb, and forbade His people all strife and contention, telling them it was better for them to be killed than to kill; and yet rulers and potentates considered Him an inciter of sedition and lawlessness. He told Edward Granville Browne, the English orientalist who visited Him outside 'Akká in the Holy Land, in April, 1890: '*We desire but the good of the world and the happiness of the nations; yet they deem us a stirrer-up of strife and sedition worthy of bondage and banishment.*'

In every age the leaders of religion and the leaders of the state have combined forces to destroy the Manifestation of God and His work. Thus Bahá'u'lláh speaks of them and their nefarious deeds:

> 'Among these "veils of glory" are the divines and doctors living in the days of the Manifestation of God, who, because of their want of discernment and their love and eagerness for leadership, have failed to submit to the Cause of God, nay, have even refused to incline their ears unto the Divine Melody. "They have thrust their fingers

into their ears." And the people also, utterly ignoring God and taking them for their masters, have placed themselves unreservedly under the authority of these pompous and hypocritical leaders, for they have no sight, no hearing, no heart of their own to distinguish truth from falsehood.

'Notwithstanding the divinely-inspired admonitions of all the Prophets, the Saints, and Chosen Ones of God, enjoining the people to see with their own eyes and hear with their own ears, they have disdainfully rejected their counsels and have blindly followed, and will continue to follow, the leaders of their Faith. Should a poor and obscure person, destitute of the attire of the men of learning, address them saying: "Follow ye, O people! the Messengers of God," they would, greatly surprised at such a statement, reply: "What! Meanest thou that all these divines, all these exponents of learning, with all their authority, their pomp and pageantry, have erred, and failed to distinguish truth from falsehood? Dost thou, and people like thyself, pretend to have comprehended that which they have not understood?" '[59]

Again He writes on the same theme:

'Not one Prophet of God was made manifest Who did not fall a victim to the relentless hate, to the denunciation, denial, and execration of the clerics of His day! Woe unto them for the iniquities their hands have formerly wrought! Woe unto them for that which they are now doing! What veils of glory more grievous than these embodiments of error.'[60]

Furthermore He states:

'The source and origin of tyranny have been the divines. Through the sentences pronounced by these haughty and wayward souls the rulers of the earth have wrought that which ye have heard ... The reins of the heedless masses have been, and are, in the hands of the exponents of idle fancies and vain imaginings. These decree what they please. God, verily, is clear of them, and We, too, are clear of them, as are such as have testified unto that which the Pen of the Most High hath spoken in this glorious station.'[61]

'The leaders of men,' He says, 'have, from time immemorial, prevented the people from turning unto the Most Great Ocean. The Friend of God (Abraham) was cast into fire through the sentence pronounced by the divines of the age, and lies and calumnies were imputed to Him Who discoursed with God (Moses). Reflect upon the One Who was the Spirit of God (Jesus). Though He showed forth the utmost compassion and tenderness, yet they rose up against that Essence of Being and Lord of the seen and unseen, in such a manner that He could find no refuge wherein to rest. Each day He wandered unto a new place, and sought a new shelter. Consider the Seal of the Prophets (Muḥammad)—may the souls of all else except Him be His sacrifice!—How grievous the things which befell that Lord of all being at the hands of the priests of idolatry, and of the Jewish doctors, after He had uttered the blessed words proclaiming the unity of God! By My life! My pen groaneth, and all created things cry out by reason of the things that have touched Him, at the hands of such as have broken the Covenant of God and His Testament, and denied His Testimony, and gainsaid His signs.'[62]

Addressing the leaders of religion He wrote:

'How long will ye, O concourse of divines, level the spears of hatred at the face of Bahá? Rein in your pens. Lo, the Most Sublime Pen speaketh betwixt earth and heaven. Fear God, and follow not your desires which have altered the face of creation. Purify your ears that they may hearken unto the Voice of God. By God! It is even as fire that consumeth the veils, and as water that washeth the souls of all who are in the universe.'[63]

It should not be thought that Bahá'u'lláh has included the entire concourse of the world's religious leaders in His stern admonition and reproof. Here are some of His words that refer to those divines whose lives and deeds justify their calling:

'Those divines ... who are truly adorned with the ornament of knowledge and of a goodly character are, verily, as a head to the body of the world, and as eyes to the nations. The guidance of men hath, at all times, been and is dependent upon these blessed souls.'[64]

'The divine whose conduct is upright, and the sage who is just, are as the spirit unto the body of the world. Well is it with that divine whose head is attired with the crown of justice, and whose temple is adorned with the ornament of equity.'[65]

'Respect ye the divines amongst you, they whose acts conform to the knowledge they possess, who observe the statutes of God, and decree the things God hath decreed in the Book. Know ye that they are the lamps of guidance betwixt earth and heaven. They that have no consideration for the position and merit of the divines amongst them have, verily, altered the bounty of God vouchsafed unto them.'[66]

Leaders of religion, custodians of earlier Dispensations, oppose the Manifestation of God, and their opposition and denunciation rouse the leaders of the state, wielders of temporal power, to do likewise. But they are not alone in decrying the Light of God. Men of learning, possessors of worldly knowledge, are no less vociferous in deriding the message of the Manifestation of God. They are savants and philosophers whose immense knowledge becomes the greatest of all veils. Some of them are consumed by jealousy as well. These men have devoted themselves for years to profound and painstaking studies. Precious years of their lives have been spent on garnering, sifting and verifying knowledge. Many of them have written voluminous and weighty tomes, have opened new vistas and new territories in the fascinating realm of learning. They are erudite and proud of their erudition. Then comes a man, unlearned, even illiterate, and states calmly that His knowledge is greater, higher and fuller than theirs. He tells them that the secret of the universe is contained in His breast. They have given years to its search, and He tells them that, unsought, that supreme knowledge has been given to Him. And His words work wonders. Beneath their simplicity are hidden depths of meaning, depths that cannot be fathomed. They contain a power which recreates the lives of men. Hence these proud, erudite men, these men of great and immense achievements, look down with scorn upon the Manifestation of God. In all ages they too have ranged themselves alongside His opponents and detractors. But they too, in spite of their undoubted advantages and overwhelming intellectual equipment, have been unable to extinguish the supernal light of God's guidance. They too have had to concede defeat.

There is yet another class or type of people who rise in opposition to the Manifestation of God, the people who do not want to use their own minds. They are either intellectually slothful, or intellectually atrophied. Their whole beings have become parasitic. They constitute the mob. Of such a type were many of those who went out with fronds of palm to give a joyous and regal welcome to Jesus of Nazareth when He entered Jerusalem on a Sunday, but five days later when told to make a choice, they said that a convicted criminal should be set free, and Jesus should be put to death. Also in the same category were those who had received nothing from the hands of Bahá'u'lláh but utmost generosity, who had seen nothing in Him but uprightness and fidelity and benevolence, and yet on the day He was arrested and made to walk a long distance to the dungeon of Ṭihrán, turned out in their hundreds, lined the route and crowded the thoroughfare to revile Him and mock Him. They were there in their scores in the public square of Tabríz, on that fateful summer day of 1850 when the Báb was shot. Whilst their mental processes are numbed and lethargic, they are incited to acts of mad frenzy. At all times they have existed, and have been ready tools in the hands of hypocrites and demagogues. The excesses and the debased standards of a materialistic civilization serve to multiply their numbers.

There are those who hate to be disturbed in their ruts. They are the smug, the well-satisfied. Whatever they have is always the best, they reckon. Whatever way they tread is always right, they believe. They are sleep-walking in the arena of life, and cannot bear to be shaken out of their somnambulance. When the Manifestation of God tells them that they are living in a fool's paradise, they become enraged. They have always managed well in the world, they mutter. Nothing can be wrong with them and their ways and their mean hopes and petty aspirations. What right has this upstart, they say, who calls Himself a Messenger sent by God, to warn them and admonish them and counsel them and present them with an alternative. Therefore they oppose the Manifestation of God. Their world of make-believe crumbles over their heads, and they see it not.

There are those who think that man is self-sufficient. They believe that by pulling at their own shoe-strings they can touch the ceiling. Man can work out his own salvation, they maintain, and stands in no need of supernatural aid. History shouts aloud the falsity of their claim, but they prefer to read history in their own fashion. In times of spiritual decadence and intellectual confusion these champions and standard-bearers of arrogance come to the fore. It is exactly when the power of faith is on the wane, and the vitality of religious belief is at a low ebb that God sends His Messenger once again into the world, and it is also at such times that denial of God is most emphatic.

Thus the Manifestation of God finds legions upon legions arrayed against Him. In order to achieve their ends men make use of the power which their position, their status, their wealth and their learning give them. The Manifestation of God has none of these. He has no church to do His bidding. He has no government to make His instrument, He has no army to command, He has no riches to employ, He has no learning which the world will recognize. Yet He achieves what no one else can. To man He restores faith, and by giving him faith,

He makes of him a new being. We should remember what Jesus said, that by faith men can move mountains. Faith begets all means. And faith is not blind acceptance. 'Abdu'l-Bahá describes faith as conscious knowledge.

The world to which Jesus came, although outwardly calm, was a cauldron seething with conflicts. His own people were deeply unhappy and discontented, seeking release, looking anxiously for deliverance. Some prepared for armed revolt. They were the Zealots. Some had, in their disgust with the waywardness of the conqueror and the conquered alike, chosen seclusion, and had found comfort in mystic thought and practice. They were the Essenes. Some, while holding severely aloof from the hated Romans, were diligently and indeed fanatically observing the law, concerned with the form and not with the spirit. They were the Pharisees. Only one section of the Jewish nation had reconciled itself to the fact of defeat and subjection. These were the Sadducees. The world of the conquerors which boasted of its might, its inherent strength, its superior wisdom, its peace, was slowly and imperceptibly disintegrating. *Pax Romana* was of no avail. Sound administration was of no avail. Philosophy was of no avail. There were many men of insight and vision who were conscious of an insidious malady, who were alarmed by the trend of events, who wished to save Rome and her empire. Panaceas abounded. Mystery religions flourished. There was the cult of Mithra with its weird but satisfying rites, and its high and strict code of ethics. There was the cult of Adonis, the cult of Attis, the cult of Osiris. There were many schools of thought. But Rome was adrift.

The Jews finally rose in revolt and were crushed. The Temple was razed to the ground. The Holy of Holies was desecrated.

> 'O Jerusalem, Jerusalem, which killest the prophets, and stonest them that are sent unto thee; how often would I have gathered thy children together, as a hen doth gather her brood under her wings, and ye would not!

> 'Behold, your house is left unto you desolate: and verily I say unto you, Ye shall not see me, until the time come when ye shall say, Blessed is he that cometh in the name of the Lord.'[67]

Jesus foresaw the catastrophe that was to come. And He also pointed to the day of deliverance.

Rome went on disintegrating. Every remedy was sought except the right remedy. And those who had the right remedy were scorned and rejected, were hunted and hounded, were put to death. The redeeming message of Christ went unheeded. Even a wise emperor like Marcus Aurelius scoffed at the Christians and attempted to propagate the cult of Mithra. It was at last distressingly apparent that Rome was sick unto death. And still the true remedy was spurned. Finally a day came when proud Rome was laid at the feet of Christ. Jesus of Nazareth, Who had no wealth nor power nor army nor social status nor learning, had triumphed. But Rome had to be purged, and Rome tottered to its downfall. Then it was that the Church of Christ could save what was worth saving in Rome. That very Faith which was erstwhile nurtured in secret in the catacombs of Rome gave the Western World a new society and provided that society with a new basis. Rome with all its attainments knew nothing of the worth and value of each human soul. Now western man became freed in Christ and for a time the innate worth and dignity of every human soul was conceded.

Jesus died what was thought to be a very shameful death on the cross. Those who brought about His death were certain that they had utterly destroyed Him and His work. One of His twelve disciples had betrayed Him and handed Him to the enemy. The disciple who had been accorded primacy over all, who was indeed the first human being to recognize the divinity of his Master, who had told Him that He was the Christ, the Son of the living God, this very disciple had denied Him thrice on the night of His arrest. Yet triumph was His at the end.

And He had none of the means which men use to achieve victory. Everlasting shame and ignominy became the lot of those who disputed with Him and sent Him to His cross.

The only true standard is the standard set by the Manifestation of God. His word and His teaching are the touchstones by which truth is distinguished from falsehood. Anything which conforms to His pronouncement is good and true and beneficial. Anything which deviates from it is baneful and false and deleterious.

Bahá'u'lláh states that in the sight of God the '*best beloved of all things*' is justice—'*turn not away therefrom if thou desirest Me, and neglect it not that I may confide in thee. By its aid thou shalt see with thine own eyes and not through the eyes of others, and shalt know of thine own knowledge and not through the knowledge of thy neighbour. Ponder this in thy heart; how it behoveth thee to be. Verily justice is My gift to thee and the sign of My loving-kindness. Set it then before thine eyes.*'[68] The standard of justice is not what men have surmised, but the teaching of the Manifestation of God. All standards should be judged against His. And He should not be judged by man-made standards. But man has always taken the opposite course. He has judged the Manifestation of God according to what he has thought to be the measure of truth.

In the *Kitáb-i-Aqdas* (the Most Holy Book), Bahá'u'lláh, calling upon the divines, says:

> 'Weigh not the Book of God with such standards and sciences as are current amongst you, for the Book itself is the unerring Balance established amongst men. In this most perfect Balance whatsoever the peoples and kindreds of the earth possess must be weighed, while the measure of its weight should be tested according to its own standard, did ye but know it. The eye of My loving-kindness weepeth sore over you, inasmuch as ye have failed to recognize the One upon Whom ye have been calling in the daytime, and in the night season, at even and at morn.'[69]

Thus we read in the Gospel according to St. Luke:

'And it came to pass, on the second sabbath after the first, that he went through the corn fields; and his disciples plucked the ears of corn, and did eat, rubbing them in their hands.

'And certain of the Pharisees said unto them, Why do ye that which is not lawful to do on the sabbath days?

'And Jesus answering them said, *Have ye not read so much as this, what David did, when himself was an hungered, and they which were with him;*

'*How he went into the house of God, and did take and eat the shewbread, and gave also to them that were with him; which it is not lawful to eat but for the priests alone?*

'And he said unto them, *That the Son of man is Lord also of the sabbath.*'[70]

God doeth whatsoever He willeth, and it is not for man to question the will and the command of God.

'Know verily,' Bahá'u'lláh writes, 'that the essence of justice and the source thereof are both embodied in the ordinances prescribed by Him Who is the Manifestation of the Self of God amongst men, if ye be of them that recognize this truth. He doth verily incarnate the highest, the infallible standard of justice unto all creation. Were His law to be such as to strike terror into the hearts of all that are in heaven and on earth, that law is naught but manifest justice. The fears and agitation which the revelation of this law provokes in men's hearts should indeed be likened to the cries of the suckling babe weaned from his mother's milk, if ye be of them that perceive. Were men to discover the motivating purpose of God's Revelation, they would assuredly cast away their fears, and, with hearts filled with gratitude, rejoice with exceeding gladness.'[71]

'Blessed is the man,' Bahá'u'lláh further states, 'that hath acknowledged his belief in God and in His signs, and recognized that "He shall not be asked of His doings". Such a recognition hath been made by God the ornament of every belief, and its very foundation. Upon it must depend the acceptance of every goodly deed. Fasten your eyes upon it, that haply the whisperings of the rebellious may not cause you to slip. Were He to decree as lawful the thing which from time immemorial had been forbidden, and forbid that which had, at all times, been regarded as lawful, to none is given the right to question His authority. Whoso will hesitate, though it be for less than a moment, should be regarded as a transgressor. Whoso hath not recognized this sublime and fundamental verity, and hath failed to attain this most exalted station, the winds of doubt will agitate him, and the sayings of the infidels will distract his soul. He that hath acknowledged this principle will be endowed with the most perfect constancy. All honour to this all-glorious station, the remembrance of which adorneth every exalted Tablet.'[72]

Man judges the Manifestation of God in accordance with his own standards, his own whims and surmises, and condemns Him because of his own vain imaginings. The standard of the Manifestation of God cannot but be at variance with the standards of the age in which He comes, and with the standards of the people amongst whom He appears. The very fact of His advent proves that man is sorely in need of fresh guidance. There are some men who have misunderstood the true purport of their Scriptures, have clung to a purely literal interpretation, and on that misreading have built the edifice of their own fancy. Their expectations are truly fantastic. Others there are whose standards only reflect the decadence of the age and the degradation of man. He Who is the true Balance in the world is adjudged in the lurid light of these aberrations. Consequently He suffers and those who follow Him suffer, but terrible is the penalty exacted at the end from those who condemn and oppose and persecute the Manifestation of God. What happened to Pharaoh and his hosts? What fate overtook the adversaries of Christ? What befell the tormentors of Muḥammad? In our own times we have witnessed the cataclysmic end of the principal opponents and arch-enemies of the Báb and Bahá'u'lláh.

The able and industrious Grand Vizier of Persia, who ordered the death of the Báb, fell resoundingly from the heights which he had scaled, and his life was not spared. Náṣiri'd-Dín Sháh, under whose rule the Báb was shot, Bahá'u'lláh was imprisoned and exiled, and hundreds and thousands of Their followers were savagely murdered, fell before an assassin's bullets, on the eve of what was to be the greatest event of his reign, his golden jubilee. The ministers of the Ottoman Empire who gave credence to accusations levelled against Bahá'u'lláh and maliciously schemed His incarceration in 'Akká, met with disgrace and died in misery. Sulṭán 'Abdu'l-'Azíz, the Ottoman ruler, lost his throne and perished wretchedly. No less humiliating was the end of Sulṭán 'Abdu'l-Ḥamíd, who was given the epithet of ''Abdu'l the Damned'. Indeed both the Qájár dynasty in Persia, and the House of Ottoman in Turkey were ousted from their thrones. These are but a few instances. Disaster befell all the persecutors of the Faith of Bahá'u'lláh.

Proof of the Manifestation of God

Christ warned His followers not to be beguiled by false prophets. He also said that by their fruits ye shall know them. How can one make certain that the Man Who claims to be the Messenger of God, does in fact speak the truth? We have already mentioned that a teaching which is false, no matter how successful and pervading it may initially be, cannot in the long run last its course. Its lie will be exposed and it will die and be forgotten. It has also been pointed out that a religion, and subdivisions within a religion, are not of the same order. But one cannot merely await the verdict of time to set the seal of doom upon a false claim and false teaching. The first test to apply is whether the claimant to the station of prophethood is steadfast and firm and unyielding. Does He withstand all opposition, does He refuse to bow to adversity, does He accept every suffering with radiant acquiescence, does He wax stronger and stronger under incredible strain and pressure, does He remain calm and serene and unperturbed when jeers and jibes and calumnies assail Him on all sides?

In the *Kitáb-i-Íqán* (*The Book of Certitude*), Bahá'u'lláh writes thus, while adducing proofs to substantiate the claim of the Báb:

> 'Another proof and evidence of the truth of this Revelation, which amongst all other proofs shineth as the sun, is the constancy of the eternal Beauty in proclaiming the Faith of God. Though young and tender of age, and though the Cause He revealed was contrary to the desire of all the peoples of earth, both high and low, rich and poor, exalted and abased, king and subject, yet He arose and steadfastly proclaimed it. All have known and heard this. He was afraid of no one; He was regardless of consequences. Could such a thing be made manifest except through the power of a divine Revelation, and the potency of God's invincible Will? By the righteousness of God! Were any one to entertain so great a Revelation in his heart, the thought of such a declaration would alone confound him! Were the hearts of all men to be crowded into his heart, he would still hesitate to venture upon so awful an enterprise. He could achieve it only by the permission of God, only if the channel of his heart were to be linked with the Source of divine grace, and his soul be assured of the unfailing sustenance of the Almighty. To what, We wonder, do they ascribe so great a daring? Do they accuse Him of folly as they accused the Prophets of old? Or do they maintain that His motive was none other than leadership and the acquisition of earthly riches?'[73]

No Manifestation of God has ever turned back. From the moment He becomes conscious of His mandate and His task, He knows that He must go forward, no matter what awaits Him ahead. For Him there can be no retreat, indeed even no halting. Jesus knew what there was at the end of the road. He told His disciples that He was going to Jerusalem to certain death, but

He did not draw back. Of course there are moments when the Manifestation of God despairs of the world, yearns for release. And it should be so, because He fully partakes of human qualities. Jesus said, during His hours of agony in the Garden of Gethsemane, '*Father, if thou be willing, remove this cup from me,*' but added to His prayer, '*nevertheless not my will, but thine, be done.*'[74] And once He lamented that the birds of the air and the beasts of the field had nests and lairs, but the Son of Man had nowhere to rest His head. Yet He sought no relief and went forward to the bitter end.

In a meditation which, in its English rendering, has become known as *The Fire Tablet*, Bahá'u'lláh, addressing Him Whose Vicar on earth He was, bewails His plight in words such as these:

> 'Calamity hath reached its height; where is the coming of Thy succour, O Saviour of the worlds!
>
> 'Darkness hath settled on creation; where is the shining of Thy brightness, O Radiance of the worlds!
>
> 'Sorrows have caught the dayspring of Thy tenderest Name; where is the joy of the Manifestor of Thy Presence, O Gladness of the worlds!...
>
> 'Thou hast forsaken Me in a strange land; where are the emblems of Thy faithfulness, O Trust of all the worlds!...
>
> 'Thou seest this Wronged One in tyranny amongst the Syrians; where is the dawning of the radiance of Thy morning, O Lamp of all the worlds!...
>
> 'Bahá is drowning in a sea of pain; where is Thy rescue ship, O Saviour of the worlds!'

Then comes to Him the Voice of God:

> '*O Thou supreme Pen, We have heard Thy sweetest cry from the eternal Realm; and We have heard what the Tongue of Grandeur spoke, O Wronged One of the worlds!...*
>
> '*... We have made abasement the garment of Thy glory, and sorrow the beauty of Thy temple, O Thou Treasure of the worlds!*

'Thou seest the hearts are filled with hate and shalt absolve them, Thou Who dost hide the sins of all the worlds!

'When the swords flash, go forward; when the shafts fly, press onward, O Thou Victim of the worlds.'

And Bahá'u'lláh responds:

'Surely I have heard Thy call, O All-Glorious Beloved; and now is the face of Bahá flaming with the heat of tribulation and with the fire of Thy shining words.

'Bahá hath risen up in faithfulness at the place of sacrifice, looking toward Thy pleasure, O Desire of the worlds.'

The tenderness, the overwhelming power, the poignancy of this meditation of Bahá'u'lláh cannot be adequately conveyed in a translation, however eloquent it may be.

The Manifestation of God accepts and withstands every tribulation for the sake of the Mission given to Him. Engulfed by seas of adversity He remains a rock of constancy. He *is* the rock of salvation. Therefore He is never submerged. By that test one knows that He is indeed 'the Way, the Truth, and the Life.'

Can He change human hearts?

The Manifestation of God always appears in the darkest place on earth, amongst people the most degraded. Where did Muḥammad raise His call? Amongst people whose law was the law of the sword, who fought and pillaged and plundered for eight months, and then observed a four months' truce, who treated women as their chattels, who buried their newly-born daughters alive, who worshipped images of stone. Their religion had been the religion of Abraham, the breaker of idols, but they had debased it to idolatry. Muḥammad raised them out of the abyss. He told them that they should have believed in Moses and in Jesus. Had they done that they would not have sunk to the level of polytheism. He gave them faith in One God, Almighty, All-Sufficing, Merciful and Generous. He provided them with an elevating and purifying moral code. He supplied them with the vision and the trust that enabled them to feel and act as brothers. He stilled primitive passions within them. Not only did He transform fierce, individual idolaters into benevolent, God-fearing monotheists; He made of the tribes and clans of Arabia a nation. He became the first nation-builder in the history of the world. He inculcated true patriotism in their hearts whilst giving them at the same time the consciousness of the brotherhood of the believers. In a miraculously short period of time these people who had indeed been half-savages, tearing one another to pieces, became capable of united, concerted action. They challenged the power and the dominion of the Byzantine and of the Sassanid Empires. Both collapsed before them. The Islamic civilization, one of the most brilliant and most productive episodes in the life of Man, owed its impulse, its animating force, its sustaining power, its guarantee of continuity and stability to the teaching and the regenerating mission of the Prophet of Arabia.

It is the glory of the Islamic civilization that its edifice was raised not by people of the same creed or the same race, but through the sustained cooperation of diverse religious disciplines and diverse ethnic groups: Jews, Christians and Muslims; Arabs, Persians, Syrians, Egyptians, Indians, Greeks, Spaniards, Berbers of North Africa. Baghdád, Cairo and Cordova, thousands of miles apart, rose to great heights. Their colleges became the most outstanding centres of learning throughout the civilized world. The universities of Christendom were later modelled on them. To them came scholars from Christian Europe. One of these eventually became the Supreme Pontiff of the Church of Rome. He was Gerbert of Aurillac, a Frenchman. The most learned man of his time, Gerbert was in turn a Benedictine abbot, the Archbishop of Rheims, the Archbishop of Ravenna, and finally in 999, under the title of Sylvester II, he occupied the papal throne.

The Islamic civilization achieved a remarkable task which both the Jewish and the Christian media had failed to accomplish. It brought together the two diametrically opposed systems of the East and the West. The monotheism of the East and the philosophy of Greece and Rome met within its pale. Classical culture came back to life with the copious translations that were made into Arabic. The greatest of the Arab translators was Ḥunayn-Ibn-i-Isḥáq (Joannitius 809–873), a Nestorian Christian. Ḥunayn translated the seven books of Galen's anatomy, the original Greek of which cannot be traced. The works of Plato and Aristotle, long neglected in Europe, once again engaged the attention of savants and scholars. They could be read in Arabic. Professor Phillip Hitti writes, 'Arab scholars were studying Aristotle when Charlemagne and his lords were learning to write their names. Scientists in Cordova, with their seventeen great libraries, one alone of which included more than 400,000 volumes, enjoyed luxurious baths at a time when washing was considered a dangerous custom at the University of Oxford.' (*The Arabs*—Princeton 1943).

In the eleventh century Christendom waged war on Muslim rulers to capture the Holy Land. The Crusades, which were to last for nearly two hundred years, began. Christians sallying forth from Europe thought that they were going to fight savages. What they saw in the East astounded them. They clashed with a superior civilization. Returned to Europe they recounted the stories of the wonders they had seen. Many of them retraced their steps to the Muslim East and settled along the Levantine coast. The channel of cultural intercourse, opened by the Crusades, was a great tributary to the main stream of the Renaissance in the western world. All this is the testimony of history to the work of Muḥammad. His message changed human beings, changed the social milieu, recreated and remoulded the life of man. By this test, too, one knows that the Manifestation of God is indeed what He claims to be.

Can the Man who claims to be a Manifestation of God, resolve the complexities of the age? This is yet another test by which we can know Him. The knowledge which the Manifestation of God has, is innate and not acquired. No Prophet has been known to have served a term of discipleship to someone else prior to the declaration of His mission and purpose. None has attended an academy, a forum of learning. Moses could not have done so. Jesus could not; Muḥammad, we know, did not. Neither did the Báb nor Bahá'u'lláh. Yet They have shown complete mastery of human problems. What They prescribe is the remedy which Their age requires. The proof is that what They decree is not only workable, but is found in the long run to be the only solution. It leads man out of the maze of his own complexities to the highroads of clear vision. Furthermore, the teaching of the Manifestation of God is universal. People, no matter where they are, what their backgrounds have been, under what conditions they live, to what lengths they have materially progressed, however backward they may have remained in the march of humanity—irrespective of any of these considerations, all find that the teachings of the Manifestations of God apply to them and fit their circumstances, either as individuals or as a society.

The Faith of Bahá'u'lláh has today encircled the globe. There are Bahá'ís in two hundred and fifty-eight territories of the world: sovereign states, dependencies, islands scattered over the seven seas. They represent all the religions and races of mankind. Some of them live in materially advanced and highly sophisticated cities; others live under primitive conditions. Their religious backgrounds have been exceedingly diversified. Yet they all find that the law of Bahá'u'lláh is workable in their particular milieu. The problems that rack the rest of mankind have ceased to be problems for them. Prejudices do not exist in their midst. Of course there is no human being who can say, I am totally and completely rid of every kind and every manner of prejudice. These are the heritage of centuries of waywardness, and lurk in the corners of the mind of man. A long period of obedience to the law and the command of God for this age of fulfilment is needed, before mankind can be completely purged of prejudice. But notwithstanding this qualification, the followers of Bahá'u'lláh have left behind them all those barriers and divisions which are the bane and curse of the life of mankind in this mid-twentieth century. Of them Shoghi Effendi, the Guardian of the Bahá'í Faith, wrote nearly three decades ago:

> 'This universal, this transcending love which the followers of the Bahá'í Faith feel for their fellow-men, of whatever race, creed, class or nation, is neither mysterious, nor can it be said to have been artificially stimulated. It is both spontaneous and genuine. They whose hearts are warmed by the energizing influence of God's creative love cherish His creatures for His sake, and recognize in every human face a sign of His reflected glory. Of such men and women it may be truly said that to them "every foreign land is a fatherland, and every fatherland a foreign land".'[75]

The "Fruits" of Bahá'u'lláh

While the world in its crazy careering towards the abyss, the nadir of its fortunes, is every day engendering fresh hatreds and enmities, the followers of Bahá'u'lláh quietly, patiently, steadfastly lead the way to redemption. For nothing can or will save the world from the perils besetting it on all sides except an invincible faith in the oneness of mankind, and the will to give practical effect to that unswerving belief. And this is one of the cardinal principles of the Faith of Bahá'u'lláh, which, together with two other cardinal principles—the oneness of God and the oneness of religion or revelation—constitute the trinity of Bahá'í belief. Every other principle enunciated by Bahá'u'lláh stems directly or indirectly from these three facts. The Bahá'ís wherever they be on this planet, believe with the intensity of their whole beings in one God, one common Revelation, and one human race. And for them faith is not blind acceptance and superstitious belief. It is conscious knowledge. For this reason, while fully aware of the tensions around them, they are not subdued or divided by them, but resolve them on the plane of spiritual unity.

A Bahá'í refuses to admit the validity of any dividing line, any divisive force that keeps human beings apart. He considers all of the Faiths that mankind believes in and practises as having had a divine origin. He will not concede superiority to any continent, any race, any nation, any class of people. A Bahá'í lives and acts and moves in the light of this supreme counsel of his Lord:

> 'He Who is the Eternal Truth hath, from the Day Spring of Glory, directed His eyes towards the people of Bahá, and is addressing them these words: "Address yourselves to the promotion of the well-being and tranquillity of the children of men. Bend your minds and wills to the education of the peoples and kindreds of the earth, that haply the dissensions that divide it may, through the power of the Most Great Name, be blotted out from its face, and all mankind become the upholders of one Order, and the inhabitants of one City. Illumine and hallow your hearts let them not be profaned by the thorns of hate or the thistles of malice. Ye dwell in one world, and have been created through the operation of one Will. Blessed is he who mingleth with all men in a spirit of utmost kindliness and love."[76]

Here is the test by which the truth of the claim of Bahá'u'lláh becomes manifest. These people, so varied and diversified scattered over the whole face of the earth, who today go forward with this fervent faith, this high vision, this clear understanding, this total and complete conviction, freely reached who constantly strive to raise themselves above the plane of conflict and dissension; who build assiduously while the generality of mankind avidly destroys; who know the meaning of true liberty, freed as they are from superstitions, prejudices, falsehoods and recriminations of a world adrift and rudderless; who act and forge ahead with one intent, one aim, one destinaion; who fear nothing and no one but their God, the God of all mankind, assured as they are of the high destiny of man both here and hereafter; these very people would have been submerged in the maelstrom of the world's waywardness were it not for the power bestowed upon them by the creative word of Bahá'u'lláh. He, the Manifestation of God for this age, said that He had called forth a new creation. An unbiased look at the world community which bears His Name, shows how truly He had spoken.

By such proofs one can recognize the Manifestation of God.

From time immemorial God has sent His Manifestations to promote the spiritual life and development of mankind. The appearance of Bahá'u'lláh, in our day, signalises the 'coming of age' in this long organic process. The Báb, the Forerunner of Bahá'u'lláh and an independent Manifestation of God, brought the Adamic cycle—the cycle of prophecy—to a close. He was truly the Gate between the growing up and the maturity of mankind, for Bahá'u'lláh inaugurates the cycle of fulfilment. All that has been promised to mankind in the Dispensations of the past will be realised under His aegis, for He has come to the world in the station of the Father. His Dispensation will assuredly be followed by another, but the next Manifestation of God will not come because the teachings of Bahá'u'lláh will have suffered corruption, not because His Faith will have become riddled with contending sects, but because His laws will need revision, and because mankind must needs have a fresh measure of the spiritual impulse and the dynamic power which radiates from the appearance of a Manifestation of God, from the emergence of the eternal into the realm of the evanescent.

The Dispensation of Bahá'u'lláh is indeed that 'Day which shall not be followed by night'. In this Dispensation God's holy truth will not be obscured; His teachings, which are the pure water of life, will not be polluted; His purpose will not be subverted. The power which ensures the incorruptibility and the integrity of this Faith is the Covenant which Bahá'u'lláh has established with His followers. In the Dispensations of the past this same Covenant was made by the Manifestations of God, but man had not yet reached his stage of maturity, and therefore the Covenant was successfully violated. It is only the mature man who can and will abide by the Covenant. Moreover, in previous Dispensations, for the very reason that man was still traversing his stages of infancy and childhood, the Covenant made by the Manifestation with His followers was not explicitly and unequivocally proclaimed. Human history is the record of the constant and successful violating of these Covenants. In the Dispensation of Bahá'u'lláh that which has overcome every treachery and has held sway in spite of titanic efforts made to subvert and submerge it, has been the Covenant established and affirmed by Bahá'u'lláh. It is only by firmness in the Covenant and obedience to it that the integrity of the Faith itself has remained, and remains inviolate, and its teachings retain their pristine purity. It is the triumph and the dominion of the Covenant made by the Manifestation of God that completes the circle of creation, and makes the Will of God operative on this earth. That was the purpose of Jesus when He told His disciples to pray: '*Thy kingdom come, Thy will be done in earth, as it is in heaven*', a prayer which has echoed in the Christian world for well nigh two thousand years.

THE COVENANT

There is a covenant implicit in the act of creation. God loved the creation of man, therefore He created him. But He did more than merely create man. God was a 'Hidden Treasure' and wished to be known. Therefore He created man in the image of His own qualities and attributes. He gave man everything that man needed for the sustaining of his physical life. And He sent His Manifestations from age to age to reveal to him His purpose. God did all that for man, and man in return had to fulfil his part, to abide by his side of the covenant. For every covenant is at least bilateral. '*Love Me that I may love thee,*' says Bahá'u'lláh in *The Hidden Words;* '*if thou lovest Me not, My love can in no wise reach thee.*'[77] God's love surrounds us at all times, but unless we open our hearts to that love, it will only be constantly knocking at the door. We must know God and love God, and know Him and love Him we must through His Manifestations. This is the first Covenant.

The second is the Covenant which God makes with His Manifestations. He chooses Them to be the Revealers of His own Self, the perfect stainless Mirrors that reflect the complete image of the Godhead, names Them His Best Beloved, makes Them His Vicars on earth, upholds Them in the face of vicious, satanic opposition by the generality of mankind, exalts Them as co-sharers of His power, His might, His dominion, His glory. They in turn have to go forward and accomplish the ministry conferred upon Them, without wavering or abandoning Their trust. They have never turned back, no matter how steep, how tortuous the path has been. It is to Them and to those who follow Them and accept blissfully every affliction for Their sakes that God gives ultimate victory. To Abraham God promised that He would bless His seed. And how blessed that seed has been. From that glorious lineage came Redeemers of mankind: Moses, Jesus, Muḥammad, the Báb and Bahá'u'lláh. This Covenant between God and His Manifestations is the second Covenant.

The third Covenant, which is the crowning glory of the other two Covenants, and their full fruition, is the Covenant which the Manifestation of God makes with the peoples of the world and more particularly with those who bear His Name. As long as this Covenant could be subverted and eclipsed the whole purpose of creation remained but partially fulfilled. How could it be otherwise when it was possible for man to corrupt the teaching of the Manifestations of God, and to superimpose his own complex dogmas and doctrines upon the simple principles of faith enunciated by Them. The will of God could be successfully defied, the purpose of God could be successfully subverted. Divisions and sub-divisions arising within one Faith were the direct results of the victory of rebellion. Many indeed have been the ills and cankerous maladies ensuing therefrom: ecclesiasticism at war with secularism, a standard of public morality asserting itself in contradistinction to private morality, departmentalising of life subsequent to the banishment of religion from the mart and the council chamber and its relegation to a subordinate rôle in the life of society, the fierce challenge and unconcealed contempt, hurled at religion and its upholders by the champions of science and rationalism, are but some of the dire consequences of man's successful violation of the Covenant established by the Manifestation of God in former times. But those times are past, and the cycle of fulfilment is now with mankind.

Jesus conferred primacy upon Simon Bar-Jona, whom He named Peter. '*Thou art Peter,*' He told the fisherman from Galilee, '*and upon this rock I will build my church; and the gates of hell shall not prevail against it.*'[78] Thus Jesus raised Peter above the rest of His disciples. It has been said that what Jesus meant was not setting up a station particular to Peter, but that He would build His Church upon Peter's faith and confession. For just then this disciple had told his Master: '*Thou art the Christ, the Son of the living God.*'[79] However, Jesus made His purpose unequivocally clear when He went on to say: '*And I will give unto thee the keys of the kingdom of heaven: and whatsoever thou shalt bind on earth shall be bound in heaven; and whatsoever thou shalt loose on earth shall be loosed in heaven.*'[80]

Peter was given the sole and the exclusive right to pronounce between right and wrong, between truth and falsehood, between verity and error. But the primacy of Peter was observed and asserted only in name and not in fact, and even that not until some centuries had elapsed. In Jerusalem it was James, the brother of Jesus, who was acknowledged as the head of the nascent church. And across the world of the Gentiles strode the colossal figure of Saul of Tarsus. At the Council of Jerusalem about the year 46 A.D. the position of the 'Apostle of the Gentiles' was well established. It was indeed St. Paul who laid the foundations of the Church. During the first three centuries the Fathers of the Church had to fight battle after battle with the Gnostics, such men as Marcion and Basilides and Valentinus and those who accepted their heresies. There were also the Montanists who succeeded in winning over to their side no less a person than Tertullian, the great saintly figure and apologist of North Africa. When at last persecutions receded into history and recognition and acceptance came on the part of the state, the Church found itself caught in fundamental controversies. There ensued a series of Ecumenical Councils spread over several centuries, beginning with the Council of Nicaea in 325 A.D. Prior to the first Ecumenical Council, which for the first time in the history of the Church laid down an exact and definite creed in words specifically meant and assiduously chosen, another Council had met in the year 314 at Arles, also at the instance of Constantine, the same Emperor who made the Christian Faith the religion of the Roman State. The Council of

Arles was held to deal with the Donatist schism which, however, continued to plague the Church for several centuries. Arianism, Nestorianism, Monophysite belief were all condemned by the Ecumenical Councils, but they all persisted. The Church of the East, as the Nestorian Church has been called, the Coptic Church of Egypt and Ethiopia, the Church of Armenia have their roots in these very beliefs pronounced heretical and rejected by the Ecumenical Councils. Next came the division between the Greek and the Catholic Churches in the eleventh century, to be followed eventually by the rise of Protestant movements. The unity of Christendom was never restored. Secular rulers and secular movements took full advantage of this fact.

Muḥammad named 'Alí, His cousin and son-in-law, to succeed Him. A few months before His passing in June, 632, whilst on the road to Medina from His last pilgrimage to Mecca, He halted at an oasis and had a pulpit raised with saddles. This He ascended and had 'Alí up so that he could be seen by the multitudes. To them He said in plain terms that whosoever had recognized and accepted Him as their Master, should recognize and accept 'Alí likewise. But no sooner had He left this world than controversy broke out as to who should succeed Him. 'Alí and the immediate members of the Prophet's family were left to attend to His funeral, while the people gathered at the Prophet's mosque to wrangle over the succession. Those who were from Mecca, who first gave their allegiance to Muḥammad, had suffered greatly for their faith and had migrated from their city, becoming known as the Muhájirún (the Emigrants). In a country of tribal divisions and intense loyalty to the clan, the Muhájirún felt that they were entitled to distinction, because they were chiefly of the Quraysh, Muḥammad's own people, and the traditional custodians of the holy sanctuary of Ka'bih, venerated in the days of idolatry, and sanctified as well in Islám. On the other hand there were the

Anṣár (the Helpers), inhabitants of Medina who had accepted Islám when its fortunes were at a very low ebb, had given refuge to the Prophet and His Meccan followers, thus endangering their own security and that of their wives and children and property by inviting the enmity of the ferocious, irate and revenge-seeking idolaters of Mecca, as well as that of the hostile tribes and clans around them. They now claimed the chieftainship of Islám.

The veterans amongst the Muhájirún, of whom the most outstanding was the aged Abú-Bakr—the third person to believe in Muḥammad, His father-in-law, and His companion in the flight from Mecca to Medina—were greatly perturbed, because they thought that should a man of Medina be put at the head of Islám the proud Meccans would refuse to submit, and the unity forged by the Prophet would be irreparably impaired. They all ignored the fact that Muḥammad had already named His successor. But 'Alí was young. These men were rich in years, renowned and honoured. The body of the Prophet lay unburied whilst they argued and argued in His mosque about His successor. Finally 'Umar presented the venerable Abú-Bakr to the multitude as the viceregent of the Prophet, and he himself was the first to pay homage and declare his allegiance to Abú-Bakr. Others followed suit. Only a handful refrained. But they too eventually submitted when 'Alí bowed to the inevitable and swore fealty to the Caliph.

Arabia was once again ablaze. Tribe after tribe was reverting to idolatry. 'Alí would not countenance any contention at the very heart of Islám at such a perilous time. Abú-Bakr was a man of piety and integrity, but the seat which he occupied truly belonged to 'Alí by the Prophet's prescription. But 'Alí would not assert his rightful claim when Islám was compelled to fight desperately for its very life, assailed as it was on all sides by dark forces of reaction, as well as by the rise of false prophets (amongst whom incidentally was a woman). Islám triumphed over the faithless hordes who would have reverted back to barbarism, and soon Arabia was once more united under the banner of Islám, ready and poised to challenge the might of the Byzantine and the Persian Sassanid empires.

But the expressed wish and command of the Prophet had been discarded, His Covenant lay in the dust. By the time that 'Alí, the true successor, was acclaimed Caliph, after Abú-Bakr, 'Umar and 'Uthmán, the unity of Islám had been irretrievably shattered and the way paved for the disastrous and irreligious rule of the Umayyids, Muḥammad's traditional enemies. 'Alí the righteous, of incorruptible nature, high virtue, sound governance, soaring eloquence, profound learning, the Prophet's Own appointee, was compelled to spend the three short years of his rule containing rebellion and the vaulting ambitions of powerful men who cared nothing for the divine commonwealth founded by Muḥammad, but only for their own assumption of power.

When 'Alí was assassinated, the military might of the new civilization was at the command of Mu'awíyih, the crafty, venomous, unprincipled but exceedingly able Governor of Syria, an Umayyid. 'Alí's descendants, the rightful rulers of Islám, were rejected and done to death, and the religious society of the Prophet became a military machine of unmatched power. As Gibbon says: 'The persecutors of Muḥammad usurped the inheritance of his children; and the champions of idolatry became the supreme heads of his religion and empire.'[81]

By the time that discontent with the misrule of the Umayyids resulted in their overthrow, the division of Islám was too far advanced to be halted. The supporters of the Prophet's House became known as Shí'ihs, while those who upheld the man-made institution of the Caliphate became known as Sunnís. Both divisions became decimated by sects and more sects, until to-day Islám presents as many divisions as Christianity.

In both Christendom and Islám the Covenant of the Manifestation of God was disregarded and cast aside. Neither Peter nor 'Alí was allowed to exercise the primacy which was undoubtedly his. The result was the formulation of creeds and doctrines, the prescription of rites and rituals and practices, the raising of institutions which became subjects of controversy and contention, no matter how near to or how coincident they were to the original teachings and sayings of the Founder of the Faith. Controversy and contention became the basis of sectarianism; divisive forces held the field. The unity of each Faith was irretrievably shattered.

But now the cycle of fulfilment is with us. The time has come when the Kingdom of God shall be established on this earth.

From the day the Báb was shot in the public square of Tabríz in Northwest Persia, the same divisive forces which had played havoc in the past assailed, at first, the Faith which He established, and next the Faith which He heralded. The Báb had foretold the advent of 'Him Whom God will make manifest'. He had made the acceptance of all that was revealed by His own Pen dependent on the assent and the good-pleasure of the One Whose coming was His constant theme.

> '*Of all the tributes*,' He wrote, '*I have paid to Him Who is to come after Me, the greatest is this, My written confession, that no words of Mine can adequately describe Him, nor can any reference to Him in My Book, the Bayán, do justice to His Cause*.'[82]

To Siyyid Yaḥyáy-i-Dárábí who won the designation of 'Vaḥíd' (the unique one), 'the most learned, the most eloquent and influential among His followers', the Báb uttered this warning:

> '*By the righteousness of Him Whose power causeth the seed to germinate and Who breatheth the spirit of life into all things*,

were I to be assured that in the day of His manifestation thou wilt deny Him, I would unhesitatingly disown thee and repudiate thy faith . . . If, on the other hand, I be told that a Christian, who beareth no allegiance to My Faith, will believe in Him, the same will I regard as the apple of Mine eye.'[83]

'O Thou Remnant of God,' the Báb had said in His communion with the One Who was to come, *'I have sacrificed myself wholly for Thee; I have accepted curses for Thy sake, and have yearned for naught but martyrdom in the path of Thy love. Sufficient witness unto me is God, the Exalted, the Protector, the Ancient of Days.'*[84]

Yet, when the Promised One of the Bayán, indeed the One promised in all ages and in all the Scriptures of mankind, appeared in the Person of Bahá'u'lláh, no less a man than Mírzá Yaḥyá, Bahá'u'lláh's own brother and the nominee of the Báb, repudiated Him and rose in rebellion against Him. Others prominent in the Bábí community did likewise. And in the years between the martyrdom of the Báb and the advent of Bahá'u'lláh, many stepped forth with a false claim, many were the pretenders to the station of 'Him Whom God will make manifest'. Although turbulent were the days, and turbulent the careers of some of these pretenders, their defection was but a momentary disturbance. Far more serious was the wickedness and the waywardness of Mírzá Yaḥyá, he who had been called Ṣubḥ-i-Azal—'The Morn of Eternity'—by the Báb Himself. Many were the wounds that he and his supporters inflicted on Bahá'u'lláh and upon those who were loyal and true; but their hopes dwindled away, their schemes came to nought, and as the renown of Bahá'u'lláh grew, the shame of Azal deepened. Even Azal's eldest son, who was to be his successor, abandoned him and found his spiritual home amongst the Bahá'ís.

The Covenant which Bahá'u'lláh established with His people and with the generality of mankind is unique and peerless.

Never had a Manifestation of God left a written Testament to specify by name the one who was to succeed Him; never had a Manifestation of God made indisputably clear in His Book the station of His successor. Bahá'u'lláh did just this. In the *Kitáb-i-Aqdas*, His Book of Laws, He stated,

> '*When the ocean of My presence hath ebbed and the Book of My Revelation is ended, turn your faces toward Him Whom God hath purposed, Who hath branched from this Ancient* Root.' And furthermore, '*When the Mystic Dove will have winged its flight from its Sanctuary of Praise and sought its far-off goal, its hidden habitation, refer ye whatsoever ye understand not in the Book to Him Who hath branched from this mighty Stock.*'[85]

And in the *Kitáb-i-'Ahd*, His Will and Testament, Bahá'u'lláh left it in no doubt as to whom the verses of the *Kitáb-i-Aqdas* referred:

> '*It is incumbent upon the Aghṣán,* the Afnán† and My kindred to turn, one and all, their faces towards the Most Mighty Branch.‡ Consider that which We have revealed in Our Most Holy Book: "When the ocean of My Presence hath ebbed and the Book of My Revelation is ended, turn your faces towards Him Whom God hath purposed, Who hath branched from this Ancient* Root*". The object of this sacred verse is none other except the Most Mighty Branch. Thus have We graciously revealed unto you Our potent Will, and I am verily the Gracious, the All-Powerful.*'[86]

Bahá'u'lláh had extolled His Eldest Son in Tablets (letters) addressed to Him on many occasions. Thus,

> '*O Thou Who art the apple of Mine eye! My glory, the ocean of My loving-kindness, the sun of My bounty, the heaven of My mercy rest upon Thee. We pray God to illumine the world through*

* Descendants of Bahá'u'lláh.
† Relatives of the Báb.
‡ A title invariably applied to 'Abdu'l-Bahá, during Bahá'u'lláh's lifetime.

> *Thy knowledge and wisdom, to ordain for Thee that which will gladden Thine heart and impart consolation to Thine eyes.'* And also, '*We have made Thee a shelter for all mankind, a shield unto all who are in heaven and on earth, a stronghold for whosoever hath believed in God, the Incomparable, the All-Knowing. God grant that through Thee He may protect them, may enrich and sustain them, that He may inspire Thee with that which shall be a wellspring of wealth unto all created things, an ocean of bounty unto all men, and the dayspring of mercy unto all peoples.*'[87]

In the *Revelation* of St. John, the Covenant of Bahá'u'lláh is referred to as 'the Ark of His Testament'—God's Testament. 'Abdu'l-Bahá, the Most Mighty Branch, the Centre of that same Covenant, thus affirms: '*It is indubitably clear that the pivot of the oneness of mankind is nothing else but the power of the Covenant*'. '*The power of the Covenant is as the heat of the sun which quickeneth and promoteth the development of all created things on earth. The light of the Covenant, in like manner, is the educator of the minds, the spirits, the hearts and souls of men.*'[88]

Despite the fact that Bahá'u'lláh's command was evident and totally free from all ambiguity, once again the faithless, the self-seeking, the ambitious joined hands to subvert the Covenant. At the head of these traitors stood members of Bahá'u'lláh's family, His own sons. There was a time when the Centre of the Covenant remained almost alone in the seclusion of 'Akká. Many of the followers of Bahá'u'lláh, although impervious to the satanic insinuations of the Covenant-breakers, felt sad and disheartened. Not content with fomenting dissension and spreading their venom inside the community, the traitors tried by every means possible to poison the mind of the government against 'Abdu'l-Bahá. And thus oppression from outside was added to strains from within. But the Covenant was not subverted. Those who would have wrecked the edifice of God came to grief. The unity of the Faith of Bahá'u'lláh remained unimpaired. Man had passed the supreme test. Man had shown that he had indeed come of age.

The passing of 'Abdu'l-Bahá brought forth another trial of strength between Light and Darkness. But 'Abdu'l-Bahá also left a Will and Testament. In that momentous Document, which has been called the 'Charter of the New World Order,' 'Abdu'l-Bahá named His eldest grandson, Shoghi Effendi, as the Guardian of the Faith. Therein He spoke thus of Shoghi Effendi, who was a descendant of Bahá'u'lláh as well as a scion of the House of the Báb:

> *'Salutation and praise, blessing and glory rest upon that primal branch of the Divine and Sacred Lote-Tree, grown out, blest, tender, verdant and flourishing from the Twin Holy Trees; the most wondrous, unique and priceless pearl that doth gleam from out the twin surging seas; upon the offshoots of the Tree of Holiness, the twigs of the Celestial Tree, they that in the Day of the Great Dividing have stood fast and firm in the Covenant; upon the Hands (Pillars) of the Cause of God that have diffused widely the Divine Fragrances, declared His Proofs, proclaimed His Faith, published abroad His Law, detached themselves from all things but Him, stood for righteousness in this world, and kindled the Fire of the Love of God in the very hearts and souls of His servants; upon them that have believed, rested assured, stood steadfast in His Covenant and followed the Light that after my passing shineth from the Dayspring of Divine Guidance—for behold! he is the blest and sacred bough that hath branched out from the Twin Holy Trees. Well is it with him that seeketh the shelter of his shade that shadoweth all mankind.'*[89]

Once again rebellion raised its ugly head. Both in the East and in the West the authority of the Guardian of the Faith was contested. But no one, no matter how prominent his position, how brilliant the record of his services, could make any deep or permanent breach in the impregnable stronghold of the Faith.

The triumph of the Covenant in this age and in this Dispensation is a fact, incontrovertible, historical. This triumph has been achieved because of the overwhelming power with which this Covenant has been invested. This is the age of fulfilment. All that has happened in the past, all that the Manifestations of God have given to man from age to age, has been but the prelude to the coming of the 'Day of Days'. '*Thy Kingdom come*' was the prayer which Christ taught His disciples. Not until the Covenant established by the Manifestation of God was laid upon an unassailable foundation, not until that Covenant remained inviolate in the face of fierce and unrelenting attacks, not until the teachings of the Manifestation of God could be safe and secure from addition, corruption and interpolation because of the triumph of His Covenant, could God come into His own. Not till then could His Kingdom come.

The Day of God

Down the ages appeared the Manifestations of God. They came to revitalize the life of man, to reveal more of God's truth, to tell man what God's purpose is, to guide his faltering steps along the path of his destiny. They all spoke of a great Day which lay in the distant future—a Day that Isaiah, the greatest of the minor Prophets of Israel, thus portrayed:

> 'And there shall come forth a rod out of the stem of Jesse, and a Branch shall grow out of his roots; and the spirit of the Lord shall rest upon him, the spirit of wisdom and understanding, the spirit of counsel and might, the spirit of knowledge and of the fear of the Lord ... with righteousness shall he judge the poor, and reprove with equity for the meek of the earth; and he shall smite the earth with the rod of his mouth, and with the breath of his lips shall he slay the wicked. And righteousness shall be

the girdle of his loins, and faithfulness the girdle of his reins. The wolf also shall dwell with the lamb, and the leopard shall lie down with the kid; and the calf and the young lion and the fatling together . . . They shall not hurt nor destroy in all my holy mountain; for the earth shall be full of the knowledge of the Lord, as the waters cover the sea.'[90]

Of that great and mighty Day, Jesus said;

'And there shall be signs in the sun, and in the moon, and in the stars; and upon the earth distress of nations, with perplexity; the sea and the waves roaring; men's hearts failing them for fear, and for looking after those things which are coming on the earth; for the powers of heaven shall be shaken. And then shall they see the Son of Man coming in a cloud, with power and great glory. And when these things begin to come to pass, then look up, and lift up your heads; for your redemption draweth nigh.'[91]

The Spirit of Truth Jesus named the Redeemer that was to come. And St. John had this wonderful and supernal vision of that glorious Day:

'*And I saw a new heaven and a new earth: for the first heaven and the first earth were passed away; and there was no more sea. And I John saw the holy city, new Jerusalem, coming down from God out of heaven, prepared as a bride adorned for her husband. And I heard a great voice out of heaven, saying, Behold, the tabernacle of God is with men, and he will dwell with them, and they shall be his people, and God himself shall be with them, and be their God.*'[92]

On that Day, Muḥammad said, men shall see the Countenance of their God, and thus seeing shall come to believe—

'*The day on which mankind shall arise for the meeting of the Lord of the Worlds.*' '*And the earth shall be illumined*

> *with the light of its Lord,'* Muḥammad announced, *'and the Book shall be laid open, and the prophets and the witnesses shall be brought up, and judgment shall be given between them, and they shall not be dealt with unjustly.'*

'I will sing of the mercies of the Lord for ever:' said the Psalmist, 'with my mouth will I make known thy faithfulness to all generations. For I have said, Mercy shall be built up for ever: thy faithfulness shalt thou establish in the very heavens. I have made a covenant with my chosen, I have sworn unto David my servant, thy seed will I establish for ever, and build up thy throne to all generations.'[93]

'As for our Redeemer, the Lord of Hosts is His Name, the Holy one of Israel,' Isaiah had also proclaimed.

Every prophecy is now fulfilled. The Day of God, the Day of Days is here. The prayer which Christ taught His people is answered. The countenance of God is revealed. For the Lord of Hosts, the Spirit of Truth, the Lord of the Day of Judgment is come.

Bahá'u'lláh is the Lord of Hosts, the Spirit of Truth, the Lord of the Day of Judgment.

REFERENCES

ABBREVIATIONS

B.N.E. *Bahá'u'lláh & The New Era*, Esslemont. Bahá'í Publishing Trust, London 1952.

B.P. *Bahá'í Proofs*, Mírzá Abu'l-Fadl. Bahá'í Publishing Committee, New York 1929.

B.R. *Bahá'í Revelation, The*, compilation. Bahá'í Publishing Trust, London, 1955.

E.S.W. *Epistle To The Son of the Wolf*, Bahá'u'lláh. Bahá'í Publishing Trust, Wilmette, 1953.

Gibbon *History of the Decline & Fall of the Roman Empire*, Gibbon. World's Classics, Oxford, 1915.

Gleanings *Gleanings From The Writings of Bahá'u'lláh*. Bahá'í Publishing Trust, London, 1949.

G.P.B. *God Passes By*, Shoghi Effendi. Bahá'í Publishing Trust, Wilmette, 1957.

H.W.A. *The Hidden Words* (Arabic)
H.W.P. *The Hidden Words* (Persian) } Bahá'u'lláh. Bahá'í Publishing Trust, London, 1944.

K.I. *Kitáb-i-Iqán*, Bahá'u'lláh. Bahá'í Publishing Trust, London, 1961.

Nabíl *The Dawnbreakers, Nabíl's Narrative*. Bahá'í Publishing Trust, London, 1953.

P.D.C. *The Promised Day Is Come*, Shoghi Effendi. Bahá'í Publishing Trust, Wilmette, 1961

S.A.Q. *Some Answered Questions*, 'Abdu'l-Bahá. Bahá'í Publishing Trust, London.

Tablets *Tablets of 'Abdu'l-Bahá*. Bahá'í Publishing Committee, New York, 1930.

T.N. *A Traveller's Narrative*, Browne, E. G. C.U.P., 1891.

W.O.B. *The World Order of Bahá'u'lláh*, Shoghi Effendi. Bahá'í Publishing Trust, Wilmette, 1955.

W.T. *The Will & Testament of 'Abdu'l-Bahá*. Bahá'í Publishing Trust, London, 1950.

REFERENCES

1. E.S.W. pp. 20–21
2. ibid. p. 77
3. Nabíl pp. 461–62
4. ibid. pp. 452–53
5. E.S.W. p.22
6. Nabíl p. 475
7. E.S.W. p. 21
8. K.I. pp. 159–160
9. G.P.B. p. 139
10. K.I. pp. 65–67
11. ibid. pp. 64–5
12. *Gleanings* section xiv
13. P.D.C. pp. 42–3
14. E.S.W. pp. 11–12
15. *Gleanings* section lvi
16. B.R. pp. 21–26
17. P.D.C. p. 62
18. B.R. pp. 12–18
19. P.D.C. p. 36
20. ibid. p. 37
21. B.R. pp. 29–31
22. P.D.C. pp. 32–34
23. ibid. p. 37
24. *Kitáb-i-Aqdas*, Bahá'u'lláh. Trans. various people.
25. P.D.C. pp. 34–35
26. *Gleanings* section cxx
27. P.D.C. p. 26
28. ibid. p. 26
29. H.W.A. No. 2
30. G.P.B. p. 179
31. ibid. p. 180
32. *Ezekiel* 43: 1–2, 4
33. E.S.W. p. 179
34. S.A.Q. chap. ix
35. *Psalms* 24: 9–10
36. *Isaiah* 35: 1–2
37. *Amos* 1: 2
38. *Micah* 7: 12
39. G.P.B. p. 190
40. B.N.E. pp. 42–3
41. T.N. Introduction by E. G. Browne pp. xxxviii–ix
42. ibid. pp. xxxix–xl
43. *Gleanings* section xi
44. B.P. p. 71
45. H.W.A. No. 3
46. K.I. pp. 64–5
47. *John* 14: 6

48. *America's Spiritual Mission*, Shoghi Effendi. Bahá'í Publishing Trust, Wilmette, 1948 page 20.
49. *Exodus* 4: 10
50. *Luke* 4: 1, 2
51. E.S.W. p. 39
52. *Gleanings* section xli
53. G.P.B. pp. 101–2
54. E.S.W. p. 22
55. *Gleanings* section lxxx
56. ibid. section lxxxi
57. ibid. section lxxxii
58. *Matthew* 22: 21
59. K.I. pp. 105–6
60. ibid. p. 106
61. P.D.C. pp. 82–3
62. ibid. p. 83
63. ibid. p. 85
64. ibid. p. 115
65. ibid. p. 115
66. ibid. p. 115
67. *Luke* 13: 34, 35
68. H.W.A. No. 2
69. E.S.W. p. 128
70. *Luke* 6: 1–5
71. B. R. p. 86
72. *Gleanings*: section xxxvii
73. K.I. pp. 147–8
74. *Luke* 22: 42
75. W.O.B. pp. 197–8
76. B.R. pp. 79–80
77. H.W.A. No. 5
78. *Matthew* 16: 18
79. ibid. 16: 16
80. ibid. 16: 19
81. Gibbon, vol. 5, p. 459
82. W.O.B. p. 100
83. ibid. p. 101
84. ibid.
85. ibid. p. 134
86. ibid.
87. ibid. pp. 135–6
88. G.P.B. pp. 238–39
89. W.T. pp. 4–5
90. *Isaiah* 11: 1–2, 4–6, 9
91. *Luke* 21: 25–28
92. *Revelation* 21: 1–3
93. *Psalms* 89: 1–4

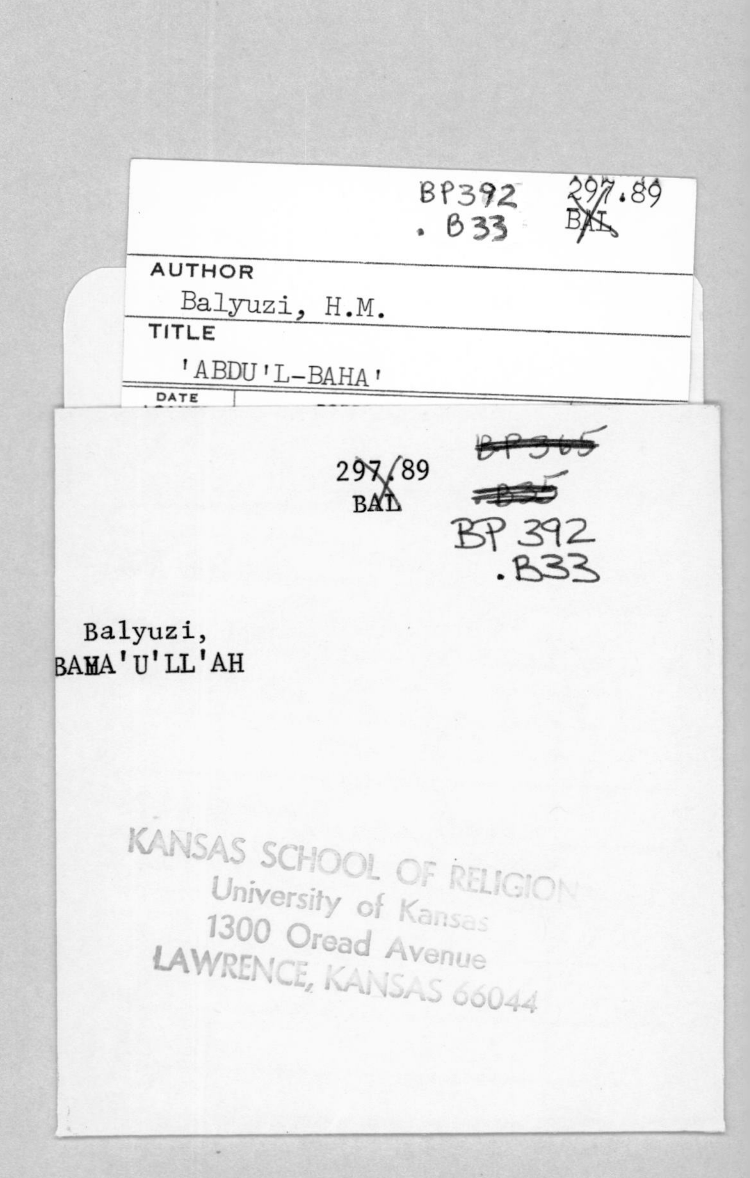